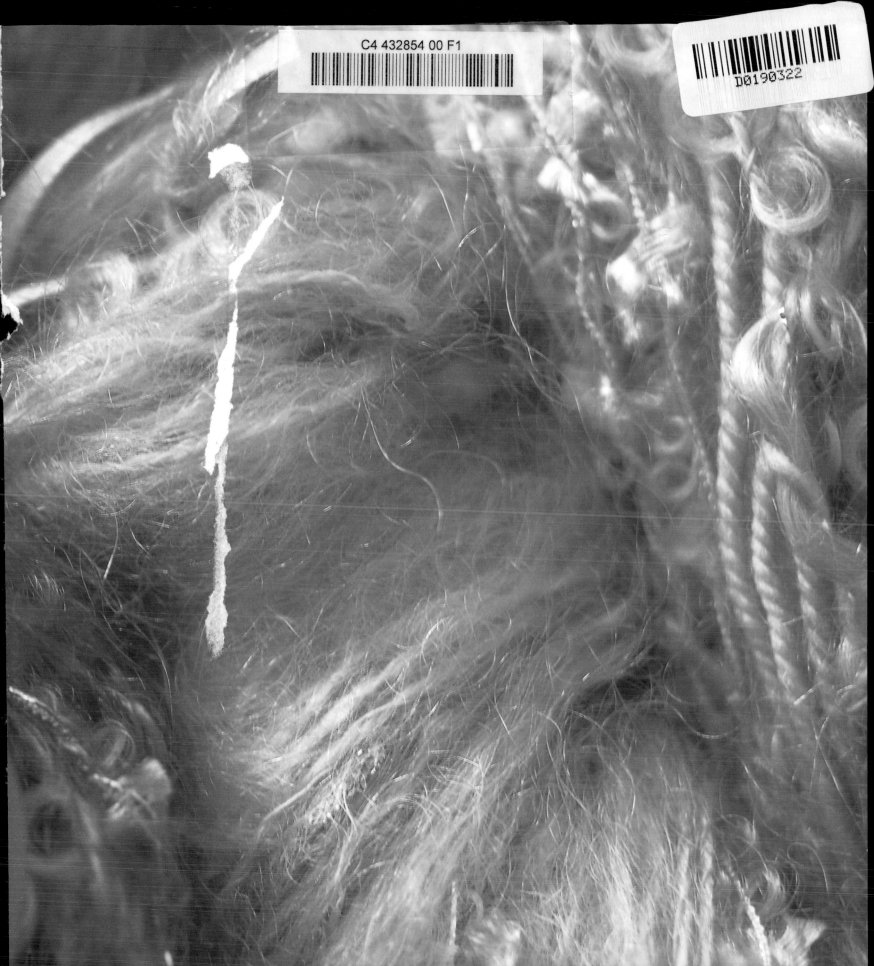

Pretty Knits

30 specially commissioned patterns

Susan Cropper

photography by Vanessa Davies

jacqui
small

First published in 2007 by Jacqui Small,
7 Greenland Street, London NW1 0ND

ISBN-10: 1 903221 87 0
ISBN-13: 978 1 903221 87 7

A catalogue record for this book is available
from the British Library.

2009 2008 2007
10 9 8 7 6 5 4 3 2 1

Printed and bound in China

Publisher **Jacqui Small**
Art Director **Barbara Zuñiga**
Commissioning Editor **Zia Mattocks**
Technical Editor &
Pattern Checker **Pauline Hornsby**
Props **Stella Nicolaisen**
Production **Peter Colley**

Contents

Introduction

Loop's customers often ask for patterns for the gorgeous garments, homeware and other objects that they see scattered around the shop. Usually, we have to tell them that they're made by independent designers and we're sorry, but there is no pattern available. Finally, now there is.

When I first dreamed of opening Loop, in the summer of 2005, it was important to me that it should be a place full of warmth and charm, beauty and inspiration – an inviting space where people could come to browse, buy, learn, talk and feel inspired by all things to do with knitting and crochet. As a knitter and devoted yarn junkie, I had found it frustrating that there was no shop in London that reflected the new-found interest in this traditional craft and the exciting developments that have consequently been made. There was nowhere that offered anything but a small selection of the amazing array of yarns that are now available, or lessons that went beyond

beginners, or knitted-up clothes, homeware, accessories and quirky objects created by the wealth of talented young designers who are working in knitting and crochet today. This is what I set out to achieve with Loop: a welcoming, friendly and informal space, where everything to do with knitting was available under one roof – from tiny vintage buttons, useful and unusual haberdashery, a stunning selection of exquisite yarns, patterns, books and the finished work of brilliant designers and makers, to lessons and workshops for all levels.

After a lot of hard work, laughter and joy, I am proud to say that we have realized a large part of that dream. The shelves are piled high with endless different yarns from the UK, the Continent, North and South America, Australia, South Africa and Japan. We have everything from the simplest basic natural yarn to the kookiest hand-dyed handspuns. This variety reflects my passion for fibre, colour and texture, and one of the things that has driven me is my desire to try to stimulate this love for yarn in other people.

The most amazing thing about knitting is that it is basically down to two sticks and a ball of yarn (or fabric, or ribbon, or anything else you may want to experiment with – but more of that later ...) and you can go anywhere you want with it, from the simplest garter-stitch scarf to the most elaborate garment or throw; it is all possible with the same basic tools. What has been an incredible privilege for me at Loop is to meet a host of talented young designers who have reclaimed this craft and made it their own. Their unique designs are an inspiration and a cause to celebrate. All of the designers who have contributed patterns to this book have a connection with Loop: some sell their finished work in the shop; others teach the workshops; or we might stock their wonderful patterns or their fabulous yarns.

Left and opposite: Views of the Loop shop with some of the gorgeous yarns and accessories on display.

I hope that *Pretty Knits* will provide you with a set of great patterns from a host of talented designers, offering you everything from corsages to cushions. Some of the patterns are fairly quick and simple for beginner knitters who just crave a little nudge to try out shaping or new stitches. Others are more challenging, like Louisa Harding's exquisite 'Cameo' Shawl (see pages 64-7) or Ruth Cross's 'Isobel' Gilet (see pages 30-5). These will both demand your utmost attention, but the results will be well worth it - they are among the things that have made us gasp in admiration as each new sample came in. There is an array of projects to choose from - clothes and accessories, such as tops, bags, brooches, wraps and shawls, as well as cute cushions, divine throws and other gorgeous items for the home.

Though it is sometimes wonderful to find a pattern one loves and then knit away, it becomes a whole different experience when you feel confident enough to use the pattern but work with another colour, or even a different yarn altogether (of course, as long as it has the same tension and a fairly similar fibre content). But that is when knitting can become a live thing, when it is fairly fluid and you can put some of yourself into the making. For example, if you're making a cardigan fastened with five buttons, you might say to yourself, 'Actually, I think I'll find a vintage brooch or kilt pin and just hold it together that way'. Or you might decide to embellish the edge of a blanket or throw with a different colour or stitch, or a cluster of bobbles. I hope that you'll gain the confidence and feel inspired to make the patterns in this book your own, by experimenting with yarn, colour and embellishment.

Once you set your heart on making one of the patterns, I suggest you read through it before you begin, to get a feel for what is involved. If there is a technique used with which you are unfamiliar, see pages 128-40, where we have given step-by-step instructions for some of the trickier techniques. It's always a good idea to practise on a swatch first to get to grips with a new stitch. Keep your swatch to refer to later; it is also a nice way to start building up a personal swatch library.

So, this book is a little extension of Loop and those who make it special. We hope you find some inspiration here to make some pretty wonderful things for yourself and others. The original patterns that follow have all been designed by people I have enormous respect for. Working with them, both at Loop and in the creation of this book, continues to be a joy, and I hope that you will love the following designs as much as we do. Happy knitting!

Susan

Pretty, Gorgeous, Yummy Yarns

'Oohs' and 'Aahhs' are often heard as knitters wander around the shop, which brims with more than 130 different yarns. Gorgeous yarns are what inspired me to open Loop and they are still the heart of the shop. Constantly trying to source ever-more-beautiful yarns for customers is my driving force. When I go to trade fairs in Europe or the United States, I am truly in yarn heaven, surrounded by endless aisles of merinos, mohairs, hand-dyes, handspuns, bouclés, tweeds, ribbons, chenilles, bamboos, cashmeres, alpacas and silks – I could swoon. After carefully selecting yarns that will eventually fill a shelf back in London, I think about them for weeks or sometimes months until the new deliveries arrive. When the truck pulls up and we see what's inside, it's like Christmas morning for us. I know other yarn junkies out there will understand.

There is truly a sense of joy in sourcing the most exquisite and unique yarns. It is always a lovely moment, too, when a customer has discovered something new when travelling – to the Shetland Islands, for example, or further afield – and they bring it into the shop to share their find with us. Sometimes those yarns end up on the shelves, too – it's very much a fluid thing. Yarns originate from all over the British Isles, the Continent, North and South America, Australia, South Africa and Japan. The choice is astounding, and they each have their own soul and character – from Debbie Bliss's subdued duck-egg palette, Blue Sky Alpacas' hand-dyes and the whimsical vibrancy of Louisa Harding's yarns to Habu's 'Fringe Tape Ribbon', sourced from a small mill in rural Japan.

I also think of the independent yarn spinners and dyers – Gina Wilde, of Alchemy Yarn in California, handpainting her silks in the sunshine; Jane Saffir, of Jade Sapphire; Nadine Curtis, of Be Sweet; and Takako Ueki, of Habu, overseeing hand-dyeing in South Africa, Mongolia and Japan. There has also been a great resurgence of people spinning and dyeing yarn in small cottage industries. They are too numerous to name, but the sheer range and quality of their yarn is an indication of the energy and excitement surrounding yarn today. Lexi Boeger, of PluckyFluff, is a great example of how far the idea of what yarn can be has been pushed: each skein of her unique yarn tells a story. She handspins her yarn and throws in the most gorgeous combinations of felted flowers, beads, sequins, pompoms, buttons, cloth and bobbles. For all of these people, their devotion to their craft is obvious by the sheer beauty of the yarns they produce. In the morning when I open up the shop and get it ready for the day, I am still overwhelmed at times by the beauty of the little gems lining the shelves before me.

These days, knitting isn't done out of economic necessity. When cheap, stylish clothing is readily available from chain stores, there is

Left: Nothing beats the drape and luscious feel of silk yarn, available in an incredible range of colours. Here are examples of handpainted silk and silk blends – Alchemy Yarns 'Synchronicity' in Silver (far left) and Citrine (far right), and 'Silk Purse' in Silver (second right), with Debbie Bliss 'Pure Silk' in Plum and Cream (second left).

Opposite: Truly gorgeous shimmering ribbon yarns can be used as an embellishment or edging to add beauty to your knits, or be threaded through a row of eyelet stitches, such as in Debbie Bliss's 'Bliss' Empire-Line Top (see pages 18–21). These ribbon yarns are exquisite – Colinette 'Giotto' (top left), Leigh Radford for Lantern Moon 'Silk Gelato' (top right) and Knit One, Crochet Too 'Tartelette' (foreground).

Opposite: These yarns are full of nubbly texture and luscious colour, from Gedifra 'Sheela' (background) to Ozark Handspun, the kookiest and most saturated colour of the hand-dyes and handspuns (centre) and Colinette hand-dyed 'Graffiti' (foreground).

Right: The cosiest, bulkiest yarns – Blue Sky Alpacas 'Bulky' in Polar (top) and 'Bulky Hand-Dyes' in Light Blue (bottom), and KnitGlobal 'Chunky' in Pink Sherbert (centre), an incredibly soft superfine Australian merino wool, dyed in natural or organic plant-based dyes. These yarns are great for everything from chunky, quick-knit scarves to beautiful homey throws.

no need to invest the time required to create something if you are going to knit with a bad acrylic that won't last beyond its first wash (though some acrylics are truly lovely – ggh 'Amelie' yarn feels like angora, honest!). Whatever yarn you choose, try to buy the best quality your budget allows. So much time goes into making the knitted piece that your work deserves the best materials. I am sure the new-found popularity of knitting is partly due to knitters being seduced by the yarns – the luscious or subtle colours and the myriad textures. Who wouldn't be? After all, knitting shops today are as beautiful and enticing as cake shops. My greatest pleasure is when someone comes into the shop, tagging along with a friend who knits, and is so excited by the colours and choice of textures that they decide right there and then to learn to knit. Wonderful!

Yarn comes from sheep, rabbits, alpacas, silkworms, goats, cotton, hemp, flax, bark, recycled fabric and acrylics; there is wool, merino, mohair, cashmere, angora, silk, linen, bamboo, paper, steel wrapped with silk, stainless-steel wire and an endless variety of blends of these fibres available as yarn. Yarn from rare breeds as well as handspun and hand-dyed, Fair-Trade and organic yarns are also growing in variety as well as accessibility. In addition, you can experiment with knitting using fabric torn into strips and tied together. Vintage fabric or ribbon is great for this and makes a lovely edging for a throw or blanket.

There are many different weights of yarn to choose from: lace weight, 4 ply, double knit (DK), Aran weight, chunky and super-chunky. In general, you can substitute one yarn for another, as long as it is a similar fibre and has the same tension or 'gauge' as the one specified in the pattern. Inevitably we've had to leave some yarns that we hold dear out of this book, and new ones have been launched while it was in production, so make sure you have a good

look around and choose a yarn that you love and that will work well for the pattern. Knit up a swatch before you begin, though, as you may need to adjust your needle size slightly.

All the yarns chosen for the projects in this book are gorgeous and easy to work with. They complement the patterns and add that extra something to an already beautiful design. They are some of our favourite yarns, from the cosy chunkiness of alpaca and wool to the shimmering strips of Leigh Radford's exquisite 'Silk Gelato' yarn made from Vietnamese silk.

One last thing – if you are lucky enough to have a good yarn shop in your area, support it. The owners will have a unique passion for the yarns they stock that a department store or anonymous Internet site can never equal. An independent shop has the commitment needed to keep trying to find the next wonderful gizmo or glorious yarn. And there is nothing like seeing the colours, touching the fibres and holding them against you to check out both the 'tickle factor' and how really soft they are. Conversations spring up among customers about tricky patterns, stitch techniques or a yarn they're devoted to, and knitting help is always at hand. Plus, you'll also be able to find out when the next shipment of a gorgeous new yarn is coming in.

flirty fashionista

his gorgeous camisole in a delicate shade of pinky lilac would be a welcome addition to any girl's wardrobe. The smocked top is decorated with tiny sparkly glass seed beads in shades of pink, lilac and cream, which add just the right degree of opulence above the narrow-ribbed body.

Beaded Camisole Leslie Scanlon

MATERIALS

3(4:4:5) 50g balls ggh Merino Soft, shade 82
Pair each 4mm (UK 8) and 4.5mm (UK 7) knitting needles
One each 4mm (UK 8) and 4.5mm (UK 7) circular needle,
   60cm/24in long
Two 4mm (UK 8) double-pointed needles
4.5mm (UK 7) crochet hook
Elastic thread
150-200 small glass beads, approximately 2-3mm diameter
Additional round and/or bugle beads to decorate the straps or to use
   end to end along the purl rows under the bodice (optional)
Small, thin sewing needle that will go through the hole of each bead
Transparent sewing thread or thread that matches yarn colour

MEASUREMENTS

To fit bust

81	86	91	97cm
32	34	36	38in

Finished length to bodice

25	28	29	30cm
9¾	10¾	11½	12in

TENSION

31 sts and 28 rows = 10cm/4in square measured over K2, P1 rib on
4mm needles or the size required to obtain the correct tension.
24 sts and 28 rows = 10cm/4in square measured over K1, P3 rib on
4.5mm needles or the size required to obtain the correct tension.

ABBREVIATIONS

See page 129.

BODY

Using a 4mm circular needle cast on 240(255:270:285) sts.
Join for knitting in the round and PM at the beginning of the round (centre back).

1st round * K2, P1; rep from * to end.
Repeating this round forms K2, P1 rib.
Cont in rib until work measures 23(25.5:27:28)cm/9(10:10½:11)in.

Change to 4.5mm circular needle.
Next round (decrease round) * K3, K2tog tbl; rep from * to end.
192(204:216:228) sts.
Knit 2(2:3:3) rounds.
Purl 3(3:4:4) rounds.
Knit 2(2:3:3) rounds.
Next round (RS) * P3, K1; rep from * until 104(108:116:120) sts [half the total number of sts plus 8(6:8:6) sts for the crossover at the centre front of the bodice] in all have been worked. 88(96:100:108) sts remain unworked. Turn (do not wrap stitch) and continue to work back and forth in rows.
Next row (WS) P2 (left front edge), continue in K1, P3 rib, knitting the knit sts and purling the purl sts as they occur, until all 104(108:116:120) sts have been worked, and then continue in the same rib pattern to the right side centre front. Turn and cast on 8 sts. 200(212:224:236) sts. Continue working in rows over all stitches.
Next row (RS) K2 (right front edge), maintaining the continuity of the rib, rib to last 2 sts, K2.
Next row (WS) P1 (left front edge), sl1, work 1 st, psso, rib to last 2 sts, P2. 199(211:223:235) sts.
Next row (RS) K1, sl1, work 1 st, psso, rib to last 2 sts, K2. 198(210:222:234) sts.
Rep the last 2 rows 6(6:8:8) times. 186(198:206:218) sts.
Next row (WS) P1, sl1, work 1 st, psso, rib 41(43:43:45), P2, cast off 94(102:110:118) sts in rib, sl1, work 1 stitch, psso, rib 41(43:43:45), P2. Continue to work on right front bodice only. 45(47:47:49) sts.
** **Next row (RS)** K1, sl1, work 1 st, psso, rib to last 2 sts, K2. 44(46:46:48) sts.
Next row (WS) P1, sl1, work 1 st, psso, rib to last 2 sts, P2. 43(45:45:47) sts.
Rep last 2 rows until 3(3:5:5) sts rem.
Break yarn and thread tail through rem sts, draw up and secure. **

With RS facing, rejoin yarn to left front bodice. 45(47:47:49) sts.
Work as for right front bodice from ** to **.

STRAPS (Make 2)

Using 4mm double-pointed needles cast on 4 sts.
Work an I-cord (see page 136) for the desired length.
The straps can tie at the back neck, crisscross at the centre back, or simply go from front to back.

FINISHING

Bottom Ruffle

With RS facing, using a 4mm circular needle pick up the original 240(255:270:285) cast-on sts. Join for knitting in the round and PM at the beginning of the round.
1st round Knit.
2nd round Inc 1 in every st. 480(510:540:570) sts.
3rd round Knit.
Cast off.
Weave in all ends.
Gently block to shape following the instructions on page 138 and referring to the ball band.

Crochet Edging

With RS facing, using a 4.5mm crochet hook and starting at the centre right front, work a row of double crochet up and down the right front bodice, across the back and then up and down the left front bodice.

Beading

Work one front at a time. Starting with the first two knit columns at the centre front edge of the left front bodice, count up two stitches in each knit column. With needle and thread, sew the two knit stitches together, circling the stitches twice. It is not necessary to pull the stitch too tight. Without breaking the thread, sew on a bead, then secure the thread at the back. Next, count up four rows in the second and third knit columns and sew together, incorporating a bead. Continue working either across the columns or up and down, alternating every four stitches until the entire bodice is covered (see photograph opposite).
Sew the eight stitches cast on for the centre front right bodice into position, underlapping the left front bodice.
The band of purl stitches under the bodice may be beaded with contrasting bugle beads or more of the same beads used in the bodice. Beads can also be added to the straps.
Weave elastic thread through the backs of both bands of knit stitches under the bodice.
Attach straps.

the great empire-line shape of this cute cap-sleeve top in a vibrant shade of teal is emphasized by the contrasting leaf-green ribbon threaded through the eyelet ridge. The 'skirt' is worked in stocking stitch, while the yoked top features pretty bird's-eye spots. Sweet detailing and gorgeous fresh colours combine to make this a must-have top.

'Bliss' Empire-Line Top   Debbie Bliss

MATERIALS
8(9:10) 50g balls Debbie Bliss Cathay, shade 07 Teal. Yarn A
Small ball of smooth contrasting yarn. Yarn B (see note below)
Pair each 3.25mm (UK 10) and 3.75mm (UK 9) knitting needles
One 3.25mm (UK 10) circular needle, 60cm/24in long
Stitch holders
Row counter
1.5m/1⅝yd of green double-sided silk ribbon, 5mm/¼in wide

MEASUREMENTS
To fit bust

81-86	92-97	102-107cm
32 34	36-38	40-42in

Actual size

92	102	112cm
36	40	44in

Sleeve seam length

4	4	4cm
1½	1½	1½in

TENSION
22 sts and 30 rows = 10cm/4in square over stocking stitch using 3.75mm needles or the size required to obtain the correct tension.

ABBREVIATIONS
See page 129.

NOTE
The contrasting yarn is used only to work a temporary edging, which is removed on completion to reveal a scalloped edge.

BACK
Using 3.25mm needles and Yarn B cast on 125(137:149) sts.
** 1st row P1, * K1 tbl, P1; rep from * to end.
2nd row K1, * P1 tbl, K1; rep from * to end.
Repeating 1st and 2nd rows forms twisted rib.
Break Yarn B.

Change to Yarn A.
Work 2 more rows in twisted rib.

Change to 3.75mm needles.
Work 12 rows stocking stitch, beg with a knit row.
Next row (decrease row) (RS) K4, skpo, knit to last 6 sts, K2tog, K4. 123(135:147) sts.
Work 11 rows st-st beg with a purl row.
Rep the last 12 rows 4 times then the decrease row once more. ** 113(125:137) sts.
Cont in st-st without shaping until back measures 28(29:30)cm/ 11(11½:12)in from beg of Yarn A, ending with a purl (WS) row.

Change to 3.25mm needles.
Yoke decrease row (RS) K42(45:51), [K2tog, K1] 10(12:12) times, K41(44:50). 103(113:125) sts.
Next row Knit.
*** Eyelet row (RS) K2(3:3), * bring yarn from back to front over needle, P2tog, take yarn to back between sts; rep from * to last 1(2:2) sts, K1(2:2).
Next row P2(3:3), * P1 tbl, P1; rep from * to last 1(2:2) sts, P1(2:2).
Next row (RS) Purl.

Change to 3.75mm needles.
Work 3 rows in st-st, beg with a purl row.
Next row (RS) K3(4:2), * P1, K3; rep from * to last 4(5:3) sts, P1, K3(4:2).

Work 3 rows in st-st.

Next row (RS) K1(2:4), *P1, K3; rep from * to last 2(3:5) sts, P1, K1(2:4).

The last 8 rows form bird's-eye spot pattern.

Cont in patt until back measures 35(37:39)cm/13¾(14½:15¼)in from beg of Yarn A, ending with a WS row.

Shape raglan armholes

Maintain continuity of bird's-eye spot pattern.

Cast off 5(6:7) sts at beg of next 2 rows. 93(101:111) sts.

Next row K2, skpo, patt to last 4 sts, K2tog, K2. 91(99:109) sts.

Next row P2, P2tog, purl to last 4 sts, P2tog tbl, P2. 89(97:107) sts.

Rep the last 2 rows 7(6:5) times. 61(73:87) sts.

Next row K2, skpo, patt to last 4 sts, K2tog, K2.

Next row Purl.

Rep the last 2 rows to 45(49:53) sts.

Leave sts on a holder.

FRONT

Using 3.25mm needles and Yarn B cast on 147(161:177) sts.

Work as for back from ** to **. 135(149:165) sts.

Cont in st-st until front measures 28(29:30)cm/11(11½:12)in from beg of Yarn A, ending with a purl (WS) row.

Change to 3.75mm needles.

Yoke decrease row (RS) K20(21:23) sts, [K2tog, K1] 32(36:40) times, K19(20:22). 103(113:125) sts.

Next row Knit.

Work as for back from *** to end.

SLEEVES

Using 3.25mm needles and Yarn A cast on 73(79:85) sts.

1st row (WS) Knit.

2nd row (Eyelet row) (RS) K3, * bring yarn from back to front over needle, P2tog, take yarn to back between sts; rep from * to last 2 sts, K2.

3rd row P3, * P1tbl, P1; rep from * to last 2 sts, P2.

4th row (RS) Purl.

Change to 3.75mm needles.

Work 3 rows in st-st, beg with a purl row.

Next row K4(2:4), * P1, K3, rep from * to last st, K1.

Work 3 rows in st-st.

Next row K2(4:2), * P1, K3, rep from * to last 3 sts, P1, K2.

The last 8 rows form bird's-eye spot pattern.

Next row Purl.

Shape armholes and sleeve top

Maintain continuity of bird's-eye spot pattern.

Cast off 5(6:7) sts at beg of next 2 rows.

Next row K2, skpo, patt to last 4 sts, K2tog, K2.

Work 3 rows in patt.

Rep the last 4 rows 7(9:11) times. 47 sts.

Leave sts on a holder.

NECK EDGE

Block each piece following the instructions on page 138 and referring to the ball band.

Join raglan seams.

With RS facing, using a 3.25mm circular needle and beg at left back raglan, ** [P2tog, P43, P2tog] across 47 sts of left sleeve, then [P2tog, P41(45:49), P2tog] across 45(49:53) sts of front; rep from ** across right sleeve and back. 176(184:192) sts.

PM to indicate beg of round.

1st round Take yarn to back of work, * bring yarn from back to front over needle, P2tog, take yarn to back between sts; rep from * to marker.

2nd round Knit across all stitches, working into back of the yo of the previous row.

Cast off purlways.

FINISHING

Remove Yarn B carefully to reveal a picot edge.

Join sleeve and side seams.

Thread ribbon through eyelet row at start of yoke on front and back, with ribbon ends at centre front.

'Elsie' Swing Cardigan   Amy Twigger Holroyd

MATERIALS

8(9) 100g balls Rowan Big Wool, shade 20 Lucky

Pair 10mm (UK 000) knitting needles

Pair 12mm knitting needles

Stitch holders or set of four 12mm double-pointed needles
  (to hold stitches)

Row counter

MEASUREMENTS

To fit bust

81-91	91-102cm
32-36	36-40in

Length to centre back

52	56cm
20½	22in

Sleeve seam length

30	33cm
12	13in

TENSION

14 sts and 17 rows – 15cm/6in square measured over stocking stitch on 12mm needles or the size required to obtain the correct tension.

ABBREVIATIONS

See page 129.

K4tog Knit 4 stitches together.

FRONT PANELS (Make 2)

Using 12mm needles cast on 42(50) sts.

1st row * K2, P2; rep from * to last 2 sts, K2.

2nd row P1, * K2, P2; rep from * to last st, K1.

3rd row * P2, K2; rep from * to last 2 sts, P2.

4th row K1, * P2, K2; rep from * to last st, P1.

These 4 rows form diagonal rib.

5th to 14th(16th) rows Repeat 1st to 4th rows 2(3) times and the 1st and 2nd rows 1(0) times.

Next row (RS) K1, skpo 0(1) time, knit to last 3 sts, K2tog 0(1) time, K1. 42(48) sts.

Work 25 rows in st-st beg with a purl row.

Do not cast off. Leave stitches on a holder or 12mm double-pointed needle.

BACK PANEL (Make 1)

Using 12mm needles cast on 86(98) sts.

Work 14(16) rows diagonal rib as given for the fronts.

Next row (RS) K1, skpo, knit to last 3 sts, K2tog, K1. 84(96) sts.

Work 25 rows in st-st beg with a purl row.

Do not cast off. Leave stitches on a holder or 12mm double-pointed needle.

SLEEVES (Make 2)

Using 12mm needles cast on 38(42) sts.

Work 14(16) rows diagonal rib as given for fronts.

15th(17th) row Knit.

16th(18th) row Purl.

Repeat these 2 rows 0(1) time.

17th(21st) row K1, skpo, knit to last 3 sts, K2tog, K1. 36(40) sts.

18th(22nd) to 24th(28th) rows Work 7 rows in st-st beg with a purl row.

25th(29th) to 32nd(36th) rows Repeat 17th(21st) to 24th(28th) rows once. 34(38) sts.

33rd(37th) row K1, skpo, knit to last 3 sts, K2tog, K1. 32(36) sts.

34th(38th) row Purl.

Do not cast off. Leave stitches on a holder or 12mm double-pointed needle.

Join right front panel, right sleeve and back

35th(39th) row (RS) With RS facing, hold right sleeve in your left hand and hold right front panel in your right hand. Slip 3 sts from front panel to LHN, K4tog (one stitch from sleeve and the 3 sts from front panel), knit to last st of sleeve and leave this st unworked on RHN. With RS facing, hold back panel in your left hand. Slip the last (unworked) stitch of sleeve onto LHN with the back panel sts and K4tog tbl (one stitch from sleeve and 3 sts from back panel). Do not knit to the end of the row. The joined right front panel and right sleeve sts are on RHN and the rem back panel sts are on LHN. Turn. 39(45) sts front panel, 32(36) sts sleeve, 81(93) sts back panel.

36th(40th) row Purl.

37th(41st) to 51st(59th) rows Repeat 35th(39th) and 36th(40th) rows 7(9) times and 35th(39th) row once more. 15(15) front panel sts, 32(36) sleeve sts, 57(63) back panel sts.

52nd(60th) row P16(18) and work on these sleeve sts. Leave rem 16(18) sleeve sts and 15(15) front panel sts on a holder or 12mm double-pointed needle.

53rd(61st) row K15(17) sleeve sts. With RS facing hold back panel in your left hand, slip last sleeve stitch onto LHN with the back panel sts and K4tog tbl. 16(18) sleeve sts, 54(60) back panel sts.

54th(62nd) row Purl.

55th(63rd) to 61st(69th) rows Repeat last 53rd(61st) and 54th(62nd) rows 3 times and 53rd(61st) row once. 16(18) sleeve sts, 42(48) back panel sts.

Do not cast off. Break yarn and leave stitches on a holder or 12mm double-pointed needle.

With WS facing, rejoin yarn to the 16(18) unworked sleeve sts and 15(15) front panel sts left on a holder on 52nd(60th) row.

1st row (WS) Cast off 3 sts [slip first st], purl to end of sleeve. 13(15) sleeve sts.

2nd row With RS facing hold front panel in your right hand. Slip 3 sts from front panel to LHN, K4tog (one stitch from sleeve and the 3 sts from front panel), knit to end of sleeve. 13(15) sleeve sts, 12(12) front panel sts.

3rd row Cast off 2(3) sts [slip first st], purl to end of sleeve. 11(12) sleeve sts.

4th row Repeat 2nd row. 11(12) sleeve sts, 9(9) front panel sts.

5th row Cast off 3 sts [slip first st], purl to end of sleeve. 8(9) sleeve sts.

6th, 8th and 10th rows Repeat 2nd row.

7th row Repeat 3rd row. 6(6) sleeve sts, 6(6) front panel sts.

9th row Repeat 5th row. 3(3) sleeve sts, 3(3) front panel sts.

11th row Cast off rem 3 sts [slip first st].

Join left front panel, left sleeve and back

35th(39th) row (RS) With RS facing, hold left sleeve in your left hand and hold back panel in your right hand. Slip 3 sts from back panel to LHN and K4tog (one stitch from sleeve and the 3 sts from back panel), knit to last st of sleeve and leave this unworked st on RHN. With RS facing, hold left front panel in your left hand. Slip the last (unworked) st of sleeve onto LHN with the left front panel sts and K4tog tbl (the one stitch from sleeve and 3 sts from front panel). Do not knit to the end of the row. The joined back panel and left sleeve sts are on RHN and the rem left front panel sts are on LHN. Turn. 39(45) front panel sts, 32(36) sleeve sts, 39(45) back panel sts.

36th(40th) row Purl to end of sleeve.

37th(41st) to 52nd(60th) rows Repeat 35th(39th) and 36th(40th) rows 8(10) times. 15(15) front panel sts, 32(36) sleeve sts, 15(15) back panel sts.

53rd(61st) row With RS facing hold back panel in your right hand, slip 3 sts from back panel to LHN, K4tog, K15(17). 16(18) sleeve sts, 12(12) back panel sts. Leave rem 16(18) sleeve sts and 15(15) rem front panel sts on a holder or 12mm double-pointed needle.

54th(62nd) row Purl to end of sleeve.

55th(63rd) row With RS facing hold back panel in your right hand. Slip 3 sts from back panel to LHN, K4tog, knit to end of row. 16(18) sleeve sts, 9(9) back panel sts.

56th(64th) to 61st(69th) rows Repeat 54th(62nd) and 55th(63rd) rows 3 times. 16(18) sleeve sts. 0(0) Back panel sts.

Do not cast off. Break yarn and leave sts on a holder or 12-mm double-pointed needle.

With RS facing, rejoin yarn to the 16(18) unworked sleeve sts and 15(15) front panel sts left on stitch holder on 53rd(61st) row.

1st row (RS) Cast off 3 sts [slip first st], knit to last st of sleeve, slip 3 sts from front panel to LHN, slip last sleeve st from RHN to LHN and K4tog tbl. 13(15) sleeve sts, 12(12) front panel sts.

2nd, 4th, 6th and 8th rows Purl to end of sleeve.

3rd row Cast off 2(3) sts [slip first st], knit to last st of sleeve, slip 3 sts from front panel to LHN, slip last sleeve st from RHN to LHN and K4tog tbl. 11(12) sleeve sts, 9(9) front panel sts.

5th row Repeat 1st row. 8(9) sleeve sts, 6(6) front panel sts.

7th row Repeat 3rd row. 6(6) sleeve sts, 3(3) front panel sts.

9th row Repeat 5th row. 3(3) sleeve sts, 0(0) front panel sts.

10th row Cast off rem 3 sts purlways [slip first st].

TIE (Make 1)

Using 10mm needles cast on 6 sts

1st row Sl1, K1, P2, K2.

2nd row Sl1, K2, P2, K1.

3rd row Sl1, P1, K2, P1, K1.

4th row Sl1, P2, K3.

Repeat 1st to 4th rows until the tie measures 150(155)cm/59(61)in. Cast off.

FINISHING

Block each piece following the instructions on page 138 and referring to the ball band.

Kitchener-stitch/graft centre back (see pages 139–40).

Join side and sleeve seams.

With centre of tie at centre back neck, using backstitch sew the tie, slightly stretched, to the neck opening, beginning at the start of the yoke on each front.

b ased on a vintage French pattern, this adorable shrug is made in one piece, starting at the hem with a lacy floral motif and working up to the moss-stitch upper yoke.

'Avril' Shrug   Kristeen Griffin-Grimes for French Girl

MATERIALS
3(4:4) 50g balls Blue Sky Alpacas Alpaca Silk, shade 33 Ice
One each 3.5mm and 4mm (UK 8) circular needle (sharp-pointed for lacework), 60cm/24in long
Set of four 4mm (UK 8) double-pointed needles (optional)
One 3.75mm (UK 9) crochet hook
Two vintage buttons, 15mm/⅝in diameter
Two buttons for reinforcing vintage buttons, 10mm/⅜in diameter
2m/2¼yds of pale blue silk or satin ribbon, 6mm/¼in wide
Stitch holders and row counter
Stitch markers (split ring and regular)

MEASUREMENTS
To fit bust

81-86	91-97	102-107cm
32-34	36-38	40-42in

Actual size

89	102	114cm
35	40	44½in

Length to centre back

31	34	37cm
12¼	13¼	14½in

Sleeve seam length

3	3	3cm
1¼	1¼	1¼in

TENSION
17 sts and 28 rows = 11.5 x 10cm/4½ x 4in over lace-stitch pattern (unblocked) using 4mm needles or the size required to obtain the correct tension.

ABBREVIATIONS
See page 129.

NOTES
Slip the markers when working across the rows.

When short-row shaping, refer to the wrapping technique on page 133.

The number of stitches changes over the rows.

LACE PATTERN SAMPLE SWATCH
Cast on 17 sts [12 sts for the lace pattern and 5 extra sts].
1st row (RS) K2, * K1, yo, skpo, K1, K2tog, yo; rep from * to last 3 sts, K3. 17 sts.
2nd row and every alternate row Purl.
3rd row K4, * yo, K3; rep from * to last st, K1. 21 sts.
5th row K2, K2tog, * yo, skpo, K1, K2tog, yo, s2kpo; rep from * to last 9 sts, yo, skpo, K1, K2tog, yo, skpo. K2. 17 sts.
7th row K2, * K1, K2tog, yo, K1, yo, skpo; rep from * to last 3 sts, K3. 17 sts.
9th row Repeat 3rd row. 21 sts.
11th row K2, * K1, K2tog, yo, s2kpo, yo, skpo; rep from * to last 3 sts, K3. 17 sts.
12th row Repeat 2nd row. 17 sts.
1st to 12th rows form the pattern.

BODICE
Using 4mm needles and the cable method (see pages 130-1) cast on 5 sts, PM, cast on 125(143:161) sts, PM, cast on 5 sts. 135(153:171) sts.
1st row (RS) * K1, P1; rep from * to last st, K1.
2nd row Sl1P, * P1, K1; rep from * to last st, K1.
Repeating the 2nd row forms moss stitch.
3rd to 6th rows Repeat 2nd row.

Begin lace pattern
1st row Sl1P, [P1, K1] twice, SM, K2, * K1, yo, skpo, K1, K2tog, yo; rep from * to last 3 sts before marker, K3, SM, [K1, P1] twice, K1. 135(153:171) sts.
2nd, 4th, 6th, 8th, 10th and 12th rows Sl1P, [P1, K1] twice, purl to last 5 sts, [K1, P1] twice, K1.
3rd row Sl1P, [P1, K1] twice, SM. K4, * yo, K3; rep from * to one st before marker, K1, SM, [K1, P1] twice, K1. 175(199:223) sts.
5th row Sl1P, [P1, K1] twice, SM, K2, K2tog, * yo, skpo, K1, K2tog, yo,

s2kpo; rep from * to last 9 sts before marker, yo, skpo, K1, K2tog, yo, skpo, K2, SM, [K1, P1] twice, K1. 135(153:171) sts.
7th row Sl1P, [P1, K1] twice, SM, K2, * K1, K2tog, yo, K1, yo, skpo; rep from * to 3 sts before marker, K3, SM, [K1, P1] twice, K1. 135(153:171) sts.
9th row Repeat 3rd row. 175(199:223) sts.
11th row Sl1P, [P1, K1] twice, SM, K2, * K1, K2tog, yo, s2kpo, yo, skpo; rep from * to last 3 sts before marker, K3, SM, [K1, P1] twice, K1. 135(153:171) sts.
1st to 12th rows form the lace pattern.

12th to 54th(60th:66th) rows Repeat 1st to 12th rows of lace pattern 3(4:4) times and 1st to 6th rows 1(0:1) time.
Adjust length here, ending at 2.5cm/1in below the armpit.
Each pattern repeat will add approx 5cm/2in to the length.

Change to moss stitch and mark position of sleeves
1st row (RS) Sl1P, * P1, K1; rep from * to last st, K1.
Repeating 1st row forms moss stitch.
2nd row (WS) Repeat 1st row, placing markers for the joining of the sleeves as follows: moss stitch 30(34:38) sts, PM, moss st 8(8:10) sts, PM, moss stitch 59(69:75) sts, PM, moss stitch 8(8:10) sts, PM, moss stitch rem 30(34:38) sts. 135(153:171) sts.
Do not break yarn. Leave bodice stitches on a holder.

SLEEVES (Make 2)
The sleeves are worked in rounds.
Using a 4mm circular needle or a set of four 4mm double-pointed needles and the cable method (see pages 130-1), cast on 48(54:60) sts.
Join for knitting in the round and PM at beginning of round.
1st round * K1, K2tog, yo, K1, yo, skpo; rep from * end.
2nd round K2, * yo, K3; rep from * to last st, yo, K1. 64(72:80) sts.
3rd round * K1, K2tog, yo, s2kpo, yo, skpo; rep from * to end. 48(54:60) sts.
4th round * K1, P1; rep from * to end.
5th round (increase round) * [P1, K1] 8(9:11) times, P0(1:0), inc 1 in next 16(16:16) sts, K0(1:0), * [P1, K1], rep from * to end. 64(70:76) sts.
6th round * K1, P1; rep from * to end.
7th round * P1, K1; rep from * to end.
8th to 11th rounds Repeat 6th and 7th rounds twice.
Slip first 4(4:5) sts of round onto a small holder and slip last 4(4:5) sts of round onto a second small holder. Leave rem 56(62:66) sts on a holder. Remove marker from sleeve.

Join sleeves to bodice
With RS facing, slip 30(34:38) sts of right front bodice onto a 3.5mm circular needle, SM, slip the next 8(8:10) sts of the bodice onto a small holder, slip 56(62:66) sts of the right sleeve onto the 3.5mm needle, SM, slip 59(69:75) sts of the back bodice onto the 3.5mm needle, SM, slip the next 8(8:10) sts of the bodice onto a small holder, slip 56(62:66) sts of the left sleeve onto the 3.5mm needle, SM, slip 30(34:38) sts of left front bodice onto the 3.5mm needle. 231(261:283) sts on 3.5mm circular needle.
There should be 4 bodice markers where each of the sleeve edges meets the bodice.

1st row (RS) Using the ball of yarn left at right front bodice after marking the position of the sleeves, work across bodice in moss stitch, beginning with Sl1P, P1, K1, until one stitch before first marker, K2tog, continue to work across sleeve in moss stitch, until one stitch before second marker, K2tog, then continue across row and complete the last two joins in the same manner. 227(257:279) sts.
On the following rows, the K2tog stitch just made will always be worked as a knit stitch on RS rows and as a purl stitch on WS rows. Raglan decreases will be made on both sides of this stitch on every RS row unless directed otherwise. Mark these K2tog stitches with split ring markers on RS and WS as you complete the first joining row.
2nd row (WS) Sl1P, work in moss st while at the same time work the raglan line sts as P1.
3rd row (RS) Sl1P, * work in moss stitch to 2 sts before the marked raglan line, keeping to pattern work K2tog or P2tog, K1 (raglan line),

then keeping pattern correct K2tog or P2tog; rep from * to last raglan decrease has been completed, then work in moss stitch to end of row. 219(249:271) sts.

4th to 22nd(26th:30th) rows Repeat 2nd and 3rd rows 9(11:13) times and 2nd row once while at the same time make first buttonhole after working 2(3:4)cm/¾(1¼:1½)in of moss-stitch yoke and the second at 2.5cm/1in after first buttonhole. 147(161:167) sts.

1st buttonhole row (RS) Sl1P, P1, K1, P1, K2tog, yo, K1, patt to end.

2nd buttonhole row (WS) Patt to yo of previous row, P1 into the yo, patt to end.

Shape front neck

1st row (RS) Do not break yarn. Slip 14(16:18) sts onto a holder for right front neck, join a new ball of yarn and skpo, patt to last 16(18:20) sts, K2tog, turn and work on this set of 109(119:121) sts. Leave rem 14(16:18) sts on a second holder for left front neck.

2nd row (WS) Sl1P, patt to end.

Shape sleeve tops

Maintain the continuity of the moss-stitch pattern, the raglan decreases and the raglan lines.

1st row (RS) Skpo, ** patt to 4th stitch after the first raglan line, PM, patt to 5 sts before the next raglan line, turn, wrapping the stitch for short-row shaping (see page 133). PM between the stitch just wrapped and the last 4 sts before the second raglan line. Work short rows between the two markers as follows:

WS Patt to 1 st before marker, turn.

RS Patt to 2 sts before marker, turn.

WS Patt to 2 sts before marker, turn.

Cont working in short rows until the 10th(12th:14th) short row has been completed and turning one stitch before the previous turn, thus ending with a WS row. There should be 5(5:5) sts before the next marker before the last turn and RS facing after the last turn. Short-row shaping should measure approx 4(5:5.5)cm/1½(2:2¼)in. Adjust length here if necessary to bring the curve of the sleeve top to just over the shoulder, ending with RS facing after the last turn. Another 5cm/2in will be worked for the completion of the yoke. **

With RS facing, patt to 4 sts after the next raglan line and for the second sleeve repeat the instructions for first sleeve between ** and **, ending with a WS row and RS facing after the turn. With RS facing, patt to last 2 sts, K2tog to complete the 1st row. 99(109:111) sts.

2nd row (WS) Patt across all 99(109:111) stitches.

3rd row Skpo, patt to last 2 sts, K2tog. 97(107:109) sts.

4th row Patt.

Complete yoke

Try on garment to determine desired yoke length. Approx 1.5cm/½in will be added to the yoke length by the eyelet edging. If necessary work extra rows, working skpo at right front edge and K2tog at left front edge on RS rows.

Yoke edging

With RS of garment facing, return to right front neck and pick up the yarn held with the set of 14(15:16) sts at the start of the neck shaping.

1st row Sl1P, patt 11(12:13) sts, K2tog (to maintain established patt), pick up 4 sts from row ends of right front yoke (if extra rows were worked pick up more sts in multiples of 2), patt to end of row, pick up 3 sts from row ends of left front yoke (if extra rows were worked pick up more sts in multiples of 2), slip 14(15:16) sts from second holder to LHN, then pick up and work one more st from yoke edge together with the first st on LHN, patt across last 13(14:15) sts. 133(145:149) sts. Count all stitches and if necessary on next row equalize st count to a multiple of 2 + 1 for eyelet row by K2tog at centre back.

2nd row (WS) Sl1P, knit to end, adjusting the number of stitches as necessary.

3rd row (eyelet row) (RS) * K2tog, yo; rep from * to last st, K1.

4th row Knit.

Cast off as follows:

* K2tog loosely, slip the stitch just made on the RHN back to the LHN; repeat from *. Do not break yarn and use for front edging.

FRONT EDGINGS (Make 2)

With RS facing, using a 3.75mm crochet hook, work a row of double crochet in every slipped st along the front edge.

BUTTONS AND BUTTONHOLES

Using a crochet hook or threaded tapestry needle, work a round of double crochet or buttonhole stitch around buttonhole to reinforce opening.

FINISHING

Kitchener-stitch/graft (see pages 139-40) 8(8:10) underarm sleeve stitches with 8(8:10) underarm body stitches.

Lightly block the lower lace section (see page 138).

Overlap the first 3 eyelet holes of the right front neck over the first 3 eyelet holes of the left front neck. Using the buttonholes as guides, mark left front for button placement. Sew on buttons at marks, securing them with a smaller button on the underside.

Thread ribbon from right to left, starting with 3rd eyelet on right side, passing it through the 1st left-side eyelet, which is directly underneath. Continue threading ribbon to end, passing it up through the 3rd left eyelet and then 1st right eyelet. Tie into a bow to secure.

Ooh, the detail! It's all in the detail, and this exquisite cap-sleeve gilet is chock-full of them, knitted in a stunning mixture of bird cable and diamond patterning and fastened with a pretty velvet bow. The soft pure wool yarn gives a great drape, and the pearly grey colour makes it a very wearable design.

'Isobel' Gilet   Ruth Cross

MATERIALS

8(9:9) 50g balls Rowan Pure Wool DK, shade 001 Clay
Pair 4mm (UK 8) knitting needles
Cable needle
Stitch/row markers
1m/1yd of contrasting double-sided velvet ribbon, 15mm/⅝in wide
Row counter

MEASUREMENTS

To fit bust

91	97	102cm
36	38	40in

Actual size

96	102	108cm
38	40	42½in

Length to shoulder

65	65	65cm
25½	25½	25½in

Sleeve seam

11.5	11.5	11.5cm
4½	4½	4½in

TENSION

23 sts and 30 rows = 10cm/4in square measured over stripe pattern on 4mm needles or the size required to obtain the correct tension.

ABBREVIATIONS

See page 129.
Cable 6 Slip next 2 stitches onto a cable needle and hold at back of work, K1 from LHN, K2 from cable needle, then slip next stitch onto a cable needle and hold at front of work, K2 from LHN, K1 from cable needle.
Sl6wyif Slip 6 stitches with yarn at front of work.
Sl6wyib Slip 6 stitches with yarn at back of work.

NOTES

It is essential to read the pattern before starting this project. It is also essential to keep track of rows and repeats. A row counter, stitch/row markers and a notepad and pencil are recommended.

Ruth Cross uses the following techniques for casting on and knitting. It is recommended that these techniques are used for the Gilet and also for the Lavender Sleep Pillow (see pages 84-7). The results differ from those obtained by the common knitting methods.

CAST ON

Work the cast-on fairly tightly to give a firm edge.
1 Using the needles for the main knitting, tie the yarn round both needles.
2 Cross the needles with the right behind the left.
3 Make a loop and pull through (as though knitting through the back loop) and place this loop without twisting on the LHN. The RHN finishes behind the LHN, in the right place to make the next stitch.
4 Repeat step 3.

KNIT STITCHES

Knit stitches are worked through back of loop.
1 Insert RHN through back of loop.
2 Take yarn outside RHN then back between the needles and pull the loop through.
3 Repeat steps 1 and 2.

PURL STITCHES

Purl stitches are worked through the front of the loop.
1 Insert RHN through front of loop.
2 Take yarn from the front from right to left in front of both needles and then from left to right back between needles and pull the loop through.
3 Repeat steps 1 and 2.

When working stocking stitch, the result will be similar to stocking stitch worked in the normal way, but knitting 2 stitches together will mimic skpo.

YO
Between 2 knit stitches take yarn from back to front over RHN and back between the two.
Between 2 purl stitches take yarn from front to back over RHN and back between the two.
From a knit stitch to a purl stitch take yarn from back to front between needles, back to the back over the RHN and back between the two.
From a purl to a knit stitch take yarn from front to back between the needles, back over the RHN and back to the back between the two.

The number of stitches changes across the rows. The RS (knit) rows have extra stitches formed by the yo on the diamond repeats, but these are absorbed on the WS (purl) rows by the P2tog on the diamond repeats.

The garment is worked in one piece to the armholes.

The underlined stitches are the side stitches and are so marked for ease of following the pattern. Experienced knitters may wish to extend the striped pattern into the side stitches for the larger sizes.

The stitches in italics are 'action' stitches and are so marked for ease of following the pattern.

Slip the stitch markers when working across the rows.

GILET
Using 4mm needles cast on 231(243:255) sts.
1st row (RS) * K1, P1; rep from * to last st, K1.
2nd row Purl.
3rd to 8th rows Repeat 1st and 2nd rows 3 times. 231(243:255) sts.
9th row (RS) K2, sl2wyib, K2, [K3, yo, K2tog, K5] 5 times, _K0(3:6), K1 and PM on this stitch, K0(3:6)_, yo, K2tog, K8, yo, K2tog, K6, sl2wyib, K4, yo, K3, K2tog, [K4, yo, K1, yo, K3, K2tog] 6 times, K4, yo, K4, sl2wyib, K6, yo, K2tog, K8, yo, K2tog, _K0(3:6), K1 and PM on this stitch, K0(3:6)_, [K5, yo, K2tog, K3] 5 times, K2, sl2wyib, K2. 238(250:262) sts.
10th row (shift cable row) P2, sl2wyif P2, [P8, yo, P2tog] 5 times, _P1(7:13)_, P5, yo, P2tog, P9, _yo_, P2, sl2wyif, P2, _P2tog_, P4, [P2tog, P9] 6 times, _P2tog_, P4, P2tog, P2, sl2wyif, P2, _yo_, P9, yo, P2tog, P5, _P1(7:13)_, [yo, P2tog, P8] 5 times, P2, sl2wyif, P2. 231(243:255) sts.

11th row (cable row) *Cable 6*, [K3, K2tog, yo, K5] 5 times, *K1(7:13)*, K2tog, yo, K8, K2tog, yo, K5, *cable 6*, K2, yo, K2, K2tog, [K3, yo, K3, yo, K2, K2tog] 6 times, K3, yo, K2, *cable 6*, K5, K2tog, yo, K8, K2tog, yo, *K1(7:13)*, [K5, K2tog, yo, K3] 5 times, *cable 6*. 238(250:262) sts.

12th row P6, [P8, P2tog, yo] 5 times, *P1(7:13)*, P5, P2tog, yo, P8, P2tog, yo, P11, [P2tog, P9] 6 times, P2tog, P11, P2tog, yo, P8, P2tog, yo, P5, *P1(7:13)*, [P2tog, yo, P8] 5 times, P6. 231(243:255) sts.

13th row K2, sl2wyib, K2, [K3, yo, K2tog, K5] 5 times, *K1(7:13)*, yo, K2tog, K8, yo, K2tog, K7, sl2wyib, K5, yo, K1, K2tog, [K2, yo, K5, yo, K1, K2tog] 6 times, K2, yo, K5, sl2wyib, K7, yo, K2tog, K8, yo, K2tog, *K1(7:13)*, [K5, yo, K2tog, K3] 5 times, K2, sl2wyib, K2. 238(250:262) sts.

14th row (shift cable row) P2, sl2wyif, P2, [P8, yo, P2tog] 5 times, *P1(7:13)*, P5, yo, P2tog, P8, yo, P2tog, yo, P2, sl2wyif, P2, *P2tog*, P3, [P2tog, P9] 6 times, P2tog, P3, *P2tog*, P2, sl2wyif, P2, yo, P10, yo, P2tog, P5, *P1(7:13)*, [yo, P2tog, P8] 5 times, P2, sl2wyif, P2. 231(243:255) sts.

15th row (cable row and decrease row) *Cable 6*, [K3, K2tog, yo, K5] 4 times, K3, K2tog, yo, K3, *K2tog*, *K1(7:13)*, *K2tog*, K8, K2tog, yo, K6, *cable 6*, K3, yo, K2tog, [K1, yo, K7, yo, K2tog] 6 times, K1, yo, K3, *cable 6*, K6, K2tog, yo, K8, *K2tog*, *K1(7:13)*, *K2tog*, K3, K2tog, yo, K3, [K5, K2tog, yo, K3] 4 times, *cable 6*. 234(246:258) sts.

16th row P6, [P8, P2tog, yo] 4 times, P9, *P1(7:13)*, P4, P2tog, yo, P8, P2tog, yo, P11, [P2tog, P9] 6 times, P2tog, P11, P2tog, yo, P8, P2tog yo, P4, *P1(7:13)*, P9 [P2tog, yo, P8] 4 times, P6. 227(239:251) sts.

17th row K2, sl2wyib, K2, [K3, yo, K2tog, K5] 4 times, K3, yo, K2tog, K4, *K1(7:13)*, K9, yo, K2tog, K8, sl2wyib, K6, [K1, yo, K3, K2tog, K4, yo] 6 times, K7, sl2wyib, K8, yo, K2tog, K9, *K1(7:13)*, K4, yo, K2tog, K3, [K5, yo, K2tog, K3] 4 times, K2, sl2wyib, K2. 233(245:257) sts.

18th row (shift cable row) P2, sl2wyif, P2, [P8, yo, P2tog] 4 times, P9, *P1(7:13)*, P4, yo, P2tog, P8, yo, P2tog, P1, yo, P2, sl2wyif, P2, *P2tog*, [P7, P2tog, P2] 6 times, P5, *P2tog*, P2, sl2wyif, P2, yo, P1, yo, P2tog, P8, yo, P2tog, P4, *P1(7:13)*, P9, [yo, P2tog, P8] 4 times, P2, sl2wyif, P2. 227(239:251) sts.

19th row (cable row) *Cable 6*, [K3, K2tog, yo, K5] 4 times, K3, yo, K4, *K1(7:13)*, K9, K2tog, yo, K7, *cable 6*, K3, [K2, yo, K2, K2tog K3, yo, K1] 6 times, K4, *cable 6*, K7, K2tog, yo, K9, *K1(7:13)*, K4, K2tog, yo, K3, [K5, K2tog, yo, K3] 4 times, *cable 6*. 233(245:257) sts.

20th row P6, [P8, P2tog, yo] 4 times, P9, *P1(7:13)*, P4, P2tog, yo, P8, P2tog, yo, P9, [P7, P2tog, P2] 6 times, P14, P2tog, yo, P8, P2tog, yo, P4, *P1(7:13)*, P9, [P2tog, yo, P8] 4 times, P6. 227(239:251) sts.

21st row K2, sl2wyib, K2, [K3, yo, K2tog, K5] 4 times, K3, yo, K2tog, K4, *K1(7:13)*, K9, yo, K2tog, K9, sl2wyib, K5, [K3, yo, K1, K2tog, K2, yo, K2], 6 times, K6, sl2wyib, K9, yo, K2tog, K9, *K1(7:13)*, K4, yo, K2tog, K3, [K5, yo, K2tog, K3] 4 times, K2, sl2wyib, K2. 233(245:257) sts.

22nd row (shift cable row and decrease row) P2, sl2wyif, P2, [P8, yo, P2tog] 4 times, P8, *P0(3:6), sl1wyif, P2tog, psso, P0(3:6)*, P3, yo, P2tog, P8, yo, P2tog, P2, yo, P2, sl2wyif, P2, *P2tog*, [P6, P2tog, P3] 6 times, P3, *P2tog*, P2, sl2wyif, P2, yo, P2, yo, P2tog, P8, yo, P2tog, P3, *P0(3:6), sl1wyif, P2tog, psso, P0(3:6)*, P8, [yo, P2tog, P8] 4 times, P2, sl2wyif, P2. 223(235:247) sts.

23rd row (cable row) *Cable 6*, [K3, K2tog, yo, K5] 4 times, K3, K2tog, yo, K3, *K1(7:13)*, K8, K2tog, yo, K8, *cable 6*, K2, [K4, yo, K2tog, K1, yo, K3] 6 times, K3, *cable 6*, K8, K2tog, yo, K8, *K1(7:13)*, K3, K2tog, yo, K3, [K5, K2tog, yo, K3] 4 times, *cable 6*. 229(241:253) sts.

24th row P6, [P8, P2tog, yo] 4 times, P8, *P1(7:13)*, P3, P2tog, yo, P8, P2tog, yo, P10, [P6, P2tog, P3] 6 times, P13, P2tog, yo, P8, P2tog, yo, P3, *P1(7:13)*, P8, [P2tog, yo, P8] 4 times, P6. 223(235:247) sts.

25th row K2, sl2wyib, K2, [K3, yo, K2tog, K5] 4 times, K3, yo, K2tog, K3, *K1(7:13)*, K8, yo, K2tog, K10, sl2wyib, K5, [K4, yo, K1, yo, K3, K2tog] 6 times. K4, sl2wyib, K10, yo, K2tog, K8, *K1(7:13)*, K3, yo, K2tog, K3, [K5, yo, K2tog, K3] 4 times, K2, sl2wyib, K2. 229(241:253) sts.

26th row (shift cable row) P2, sl2wyif, P2, [P8, yo, P2tog] 4 times, P8, *P1(7:13)*, P3, yo, P2tog, P8, yo, P2tog, P3, yo, P2, sl2wyif, P2, *P2tog*, P1, [P9, P2tog] 6 times, P2tog, P2, sl2wyif, P2, yo, P3, yo, P2tog, P8, yo, P2tog, P3, *P1(7:13)*, P8, [yo, P2tog, P8] 4 times, P2, sl2wyif, P2. 223(235:247) sts.

27th row (cable row) *Cable 6*, [K3, K2tog, yo, K5] 4 times, K3, K2tog, yo, K3, *K1(7:13)*, K8, K2tog, yo, K9, *cable 6*, K2, [K3, yo, K3, yo, K2, K2tog] 6 times, K1, *cable 6*, K9, K2tog, yo, K8, *K1(7:13)*, K3, K2tog, yo, K3, [K5, K2tog, yo, K3] 4 times, *cable 6*. 229(241:253) sts.

28th row P6, [P8, P2tog, yo] 4 times, P8, *P1(7:13)*, P3, P2tog, yo, P8, yo, P2tog, P12, [P9, P2tog] 6 times, P11, P2tog, yo, P8, P2tog, yo, P3, *P1(7:13)*, P8, [P2tog, yo, P8] 4 times, P6. 223(235:247) sts.

29th row (decrease row) K2, sl2wyib, K2, [K3, yo, K2tog, K5] 4 times, K3, yo, K2tog, K2, *K0(3:6), sl1wyib, K2tog, psso, K0(3:6)*, K7, yo, K2tog, K9, K2, sl2wyib K4, [K2, yo, K5, yo, K1, K2tog] 6 times, K3, sl2wyib, K11, yo, K2tog, K7, *K0(3:6), sl1wyib, K2tog, psso, K0(3:6)*, K2, yo, K2tog, K3, [K5, yo, K2tog, K3] 4 times, K2, sl2wyif K2. 225(237:249) sts.

30th row (shift cable row) P2, sl2wyif, P2, [P8, yo, P2tog] 4 times, P7, *P1(7:13)*, P2, yo, P2tog, P8, yo, P2tog, P4, yo, P2, sl2wyif, P2, *P2tog*, [P9, P2tog] 5 times, P9, *P3tog*, P2, sl2wyif, P2, yo, P4, yo, P2tog, P8, yo, P2tog, P2, *P1(7:13)*, P7, [yo, P2tog, P8] 4 times, P2, sl2wyif, P2. 219(231:243) sts.

31st row (cable row) *Cable 6*, [K3, K2tog, yo, K5] 4 times, K3, K2tog, yo, K2, *K1(7:13)*, K7, K2tog, yo, K8, K2tog, yo, *cable 6*, K1, [K1, yo, K7, yo, K2tog] 6 times, *cable 6*, K2tog, yo, K8, K2tog, yo, K7, *K1(7:13)*, K2, K2tog, yo, K3, [K5, K2tog, yo, K3] 4 times, *cable 6*. 225(237:249) sts.

32nd row P6, [P8, P2tog, yo] 4 times, P7, *P1(7:13)*, P2, P2tog, yo, P8, P2tog, yo, P12, [P9, P2tog] 6 times, P11, P2tog, yo, P8, P2tog, yo, P2, *P1(7:13)*, P7, [P2tog, yo, P8] 4 times, P6. 219(231:243) sts.

9th to 32nd rows set the pattern and position of the side shapings.

Maintaining the continuity of the pattern, continue as follows. Read all the instructions carefully before continuing. The instructions are given individually but all are carried out at the same time.

SIDE SHAPINGS

Decrease 2 sts on every 7th row on each side of the gilet, using the marker placed on the 9th row and the decreases already made as a guide. On RS rows sl1wyib, K2tog, psso. On WS rows sl1wyif, P2tog, psso. Decreases were made on rows 15, 22 and 29.

More deceases are made on rows 36, 43, 50, 57, 64, 71, 78, 85, 36, 43, 50, 57, 64, 71, 78 and 85.

Increase 2 sts on every 4th row on each side of the gilet, using the marker placed on the 9th row as a guide.

For all increases, work to the marked stitch, yo, P1, yo.

Increases are made on rows 90, 94, 98, 102, 106, 110, 114, 118, 122, 126, 130 and 134.

BACK DIAMOND-PATTERN PANEL

As the cables shift towards the centre back, it will not be possible to work full diamonds. Work half a diamond, with the diamond edge towards the centre back and the straight half-diamond edge towards the cable. This will also prevent the diamond pattern from interfering with the P2tog decreases to shift the cable.

CABLE SHIFT

The cable on each side of the back diamond pattern panel shifts inwards one place by making a yo on the outside of it and a P2tog on the inside on every 4th row.

Cable shifts were made on rows 10, 14, 18, 22, 26 and 30.

Further cable shifts are made on rows 34, 38, 42, 46, 50, 54, 58, 62, 66, 70, 74, 78, 82, 86, 90, 94, 98, 102, 106, 110, 114, 118, 122, 126, 130, 134, 138, 142, 146 and 150.

On 150th row work the decreases inside the cables as sl1wyif, P2tog, psso so that only one stitch remains between the cables.

The cable later shifts outwards one place by making a K2tog or P2tog on the outside of it and a yo on the inside.

Cable shifts are made on rows 162 to 190 except rows 185, 187 and 189.

162nd to 164th rows On RS rows work the stitches between the cables as knit stitches. On WS rows work the stitches between the cables as purl stitches.

165th row Work the stitches between the cables as yo, K1, [K1, P1] twice, K2, yo.

166th row Work the stitches between the cables as yo, P9, yo.

167th row Work the stitches between the cables as yo, K1, [K1, P1] 4 times, K2, yo.

168th row Work the stitches between the cables as yo, P13, yo. Continue in patt until the 194th row has been worked.

195th row Patt to 26 sts before the centre stitch, cast off 53 sts, patt to end. 19(21:23) sts on each side.

BUTTONHOLES

111th row (RS) Patt 6, make a buttonhole over 3 stitches as described on pages 84-7, patt to last 10 sts, make second buttonhole, patt to end.

SHAPE FRONT NECK

Decrease one stitch inside the cable edge. On RS rows work K2tog. On WS rows work P2tog.

Decreases are made on rows 114, 117, 121, 124, 128, 131, 135, 138, 142, 145, 149, 152, 156, 159, 163, 166, 170, 173, 177, 180, 184, 187 and 191.

ARMHOLES

91cm/36in size

139th row Patt to 4 sts before the first marked centre side stitch, cast off 9 sts, patt to 4 sts before the second marked centre side stitch, cast off 9 sts, patt to end.

Sizes 97 and 102cm/38 and 40in

137th row Patt to 4(5) sts before the first marked centre side stitch, cast off 9(11) sts, patt to 4(5) sts before the second marked centre side stitch, cast off 9(11) sts, patt to end.

All sizes

Work on each piece separately.

Shape armholes

Cont in patt decreasing one stitch at armhole edges inside 2 edge stitches. On RS rows work K2tog. On WS rows work P2tog.

Sizes 97 and 102cm/38 and 40in

Decreases are made on the 139th row.

All sizes

Decreases are made on rows 142, 145, 148, 151, 154, 157, 160, 168, 174 and 180.

Fronts

Decreases are made on the 186th row.

Cont in patt without shaping until the 195th row has been worked. 19(21:23) sts.

SHOULDERS

Left back shoulder and right front shoulder

196th row Patt 19(21:23) sts.

197th row Patt 13 sts, turn.

198th row Sl6wyif, patt 7

Cast off all stitches purlways.

Right back shoulder and left front shoulder

196th row Patt 13 sts, turn.

197th row Sl6wyib, patt 7.

Cast off all stitches knitways.

SLEEVES

Using 4mm needles cast on 74(76:78) sts.

1st row * K1, P1; rep from * to end.

2nd row Purl.

3rd row Repeat 1st row.

4th row P1, yo, purl to last st, yo, P1. 76(78:80) sts.

5th row K1, * K1, P1; rep from * to last st, K1.

6th row Purl.

7th row Repeat 5th row.

8th row Purl.

9th row K7(8:9), [yo, K2tog, K8] 3 times, yo, K2tog, [K8, yo, K2tog] 3 times, K7(8:9).

10th row P1, yo, P1(2:3), [yo, P2tog, P8] 7 times, yo, P2tog, P1, yo, P1(2:3). 78(80:82) sts.

11th row [K8, K2tog, yo] 7 times, K8.

12th row P3, [P2tog, yo, P8] 7 times, P2tog, yo, P3.

13th row [K8, yo K2tog] 7 times, K8.

14th row P3, [yo, P2tog, P8] 7 times, yo, P2tog, P3.

Continue in pattern as established increasing 1 stitch at both ends on rows 16, 22, 28 and 34. 86(88:90) sts.

36th row Cast off 3(3:4) sts knitways, patt to end. 83(85:86) sts.

37th row Cast off 4(4:5) sts, patt to end. 79(81:81) sts.

38th row P1, P2tog, patt to last 3 sts, P2tog, P1. 77(79:79) sts.

39th row K1, K2tog, patt to last 3 sts, K2tog, K1. 75(77:77) sts.

40th to 51st rows Repeat 38th and 39th rows 6 times. 51(53:53) sts.

52nd row P1, sl1wyif, P2tog, psso, patt to last 4 sts, sl1wyif, P2tog, psso, P1. 47(49:49) sts.

53rd row K1, sl1wyib, K2tog, psso, patt to last 4 sts, sl1wyif, K2tog, psso, K1. 43(45:45) sts.

54th to 62nd rows Repeat 52nd and 53rd rows 4 times and 52nd row once. 7(9:9) sts.

Cast off purlways.

FINISHING

Block each piece following the instructions on page 138 and referring to the ball band.

Join shoulder seams.

Insert sleeves and join underarm seams.

Insert ribbon through buttonholes.

Now pour yourself a glass of wine!

a stunning yoke of knitted ribbon, with silk, velvet, satin and vintage lace intertwined and sewn down afterwards, elevates this simple mini dress into a true fashion statement. As long as you follow the basic instructions for the shaping and measurements, you can play around with as many yarns as you like in the yoke. Or make the basic shift in one yarn, ignoring the instructions to swap yarns, and sew on the decoration afterwards.

'Maude' Ruffle Dress   Claire Montgomerie

MATERIALS
10(11:12) 50g balls Alchemy Synchronicity, shade 76e Citrine. Yarn A
Approximately 35m/38yds Habu Fringe Tape Ribbon, shade Pale Pink. Yarn B
Pair 4.5mm (UK 7) knitting needles
One 4.5mm (UK 7) circular needle, 80cm/31½in long
Set of 4.5mm (UK 7) double-pointed needles
Stitch holders
Row counter
Assorted ribbons and/or buttons to decorate
Button to fasten, approximately 1cm/⅜in diameter

MEASUREMENTS
To fit bust

86	91	97cm
34	36	38in

Actual size

88	94	100cm
35	37	39¼in

Finished length

87	87	87cm
34½	34½	34½in

Sleeve seam length

2	2	2cm
¾	¾	¾in

TENSION
21 sts and 30 rows = 10cm/4in square measured over stocking stitch using Alchemy Synchronicity (Yarn A) and 4.5mm needles or the size required to obtain the correct tension.

ABBREVIATIONS
See page 129.

fur st Fur stitch. Worked on RS rows. Knit the next stitch without letting it drop off the LHN, bring the yarn forward between the needles, pass the yarn around your thumb or a piece of cardboard to make a loop approx 2cm/¾in long (or the desired length), take the yarn back between the needles, knit the stitch on the LHN again, this time completing it and letting it drop off the needle. Pass the first loop of the stitch just knitted (now on the RHN) over the second loop of the stitch just knitted and off the needle to secure stitch.

NOTES
When working with the Habu ribbon, work slowly and evenly, as it is very easy to knit through the tape instead of the stitch, snagging the ribbon and making the knitting messy and hard to work.

Slip the markers when working the rounds.

When short-row shaping, refer to the wrapping technique on page 133.

WORKING THE RUFFLE

The yoke of the dress is worked in quite a random, experimental way, but the exact pattern used for the dress shown here has been written. The type of stitch varies along a row, with knit, purl and fur stitch all used along some rows to try to show off the ribbon to best effect. It is a mixture of stranding (also known as Fair Isle) and intarsia techniques, with some parts having the unused yarn carried along the back of the work (stranding) and some parts having separate twists of yarn used for each section of colour (intarsia). Because this is not a regular way of working and because a mixture of stitches is used within these sections, a chart has not been written as would happen with Fair Isle or intarsia techniques. The instructions have been written in words. This may take some getting used to, but it also allows for interpretation and experimentation by the knitter.

SKIRT

Using a 4.5mm circular needle and Yarn A cast on 210(220:230) sts. Join for knitting in the round.

1st round PM to mark beg of round, K105(110:115) sts, PM to mark side stitch, knit to end.

2nd round Purl.

Repeating these 2 rounds forms garter stitch.

Work 4 more rounds in g-st.

7th and 8th rounds Knit.

Repeating these 2 rounds forms stocking stitch.

Next round (decrease round) * Knit to the stitch before the marker, K2tog, PM; rep from * once. 208(218:228) sts.

Cont in st-st, dec 2 sts on every foll 10th round as established to 186(198:210) sts.

Cont in st-st without shaping until work measures 69cm/27in from cast-on edge.

BACK

Divide for back and front

Cont working in rows on straight 4.5mm needles for back armhole shaping.

1st row (RS) Cast off 3 sts, knit to marker and work on these 90(96:102) sts for the back. Place rem 93(99:105) sts on a holder for the front.

2nd row Cast off 3 sts, purl to end. 87(93:99) sts.

Cont in st-st.

Cast off 3 sts at beg of next 2 rows. 81(87:93) sts.

Dec 1 st at both ends of next 3 rows and on 3 foll alt rows 69(75:81) sts.

Cont in st-st without shaping until armhole measures 7.5cm/3in, ending with a WS row.

Shape neck (keyhole neckline)

Next row (RS) K33(36:39), cast off 3 sts, K32(35:39) sts.

Turn and work on second set of 33(36:39) sts for left back neck.

Leave first set of 33(36:39) sts on a holder.

Cast off 1 st at neck edge on foll 4 alt rows 29(32:35) sts.

Cont in st-st without shaping until armhole measures 14cm/5½in, ending with a WS row.

Inc 1 st at neck edge on next row, on 2 foll 4th rows, then on foll 2 alt rows. 34(37:40) sts.

Cont in st-st until armhole measures 18cm/7in, ending with a RS row.

Shape left back shoulder

Cast off 4(5:6) sts at beg of next row and 5(5:6) sts at beg of foll alt row. 25(27:28) sts.

Next row (RS) Cast off 20(21:22) sts, knit to end. 5(6:6) sts.

Purl one row.

Cast off rem sts.

Rejoin Yarn A to 33(36:39) sts left on a holder for right side of back neck.

Work to match left side of back neck, reversing shaping.

FRONT

With RS facing rejoin Yarn A to the 93(99:105) sts left on a holder for the front.

Shape armhole for the dress without ribbon

Cont in st-st.

Cast off 3 sts at beg of next 4 rows. 81(87:93) sts.

Dec 1 st at both ends of next 3 rows and on 3 foll alt rows 69(75:81) sts.

Beg with a purl row work 19 rows st-st without shaping. 32 rows for armhole worked in all.

Cont as for dress with ribbon, starting at the 1st row of front neck shaping and using Yarn A throughout.

Shape armhole for the dress with ribbon

Work the armhole shaping at the same time as knitting in the ribbon. Each time the new yarn is added, tie it in as for a stripe or for multicoloured knitting, either carrying the unused yarn along the back of the work, or using a different ball for each section, twisting the yarn together at the colour change as for intarsia.

Cont in st-st.

1st row (RS) Using Yarn A cast off 3 sts, knit to end. 90(96:102) sts.

2nd row Using Yarn A cast off 3 sts, purl to end. 87(93:99) sts.

3rd row Using Yarn A cast off 3 sts, K25(28:31), join Yarn B and K1, (fur st 1, K1) 3 times, return to Yarn A and knit to end. 84(90:96) sts.

4th row Using Yarn A cast off 3 sts, P16(19:22), change to Yarn B and K15, return to Yarn A and purl to end. 81(87:93) sts.

5th row Using Yarn A dec 1 st at beg of row, knit to 1 st before Yarn B of previous row, change to Yarn B and K20, return to Yarn A and knit to end, decreasing 1 st at end of row. 79(85:91) sts.

6th row Using Yarn A dec 1 st at beg of row, purl to first Yarn B st of previous row, change to Yarn B and K25, return to Yarn A and purl to end, decreasing 1 st at end of row. 77(83:89) sts.

7th row Using Yarn A dec 1 st at beg of row, K28(31:34), change to Yarn B and K1, (fur st 1, K1) 4 times, return to Yarn A and knit to end, decreasing 1 st at end of row. 75(81:87) sts.

8th row Using Yarn A, purl.

9th row Using Yarn A, knit, dec 1 st at both ends of the row. 73(79:85) sts.

10th row Using Yarn A, purl.

11th row Using Yarn A, dec 1 st at beg of row, K5(8:11), change to Yarn B and K14, return to Yarn A and knit to end, decreasing 1 st at end of row. 71(77:83) sts.

12th row Using Yarn A, purl to 1 st before Yarn B of previous row, change to Yarn B and K16, return to Yarn A and purl to end of row.

13th row Using Yarn A dec 1 st at beg of row, K8(11:14), change to Yarn B and K10, return to Yarn A and knit to end of row, decreasing 1 st at end of row 69(75:81) sts.

14th to 16th rows Using Yarn A work 3 rows st-st without shaping.

17th row Using Yarn A K20(23:26), change to Yarn B and K5, (fur st 1, K1) 10 times, K5, return to Yarn A and knit to end.

18th row Using Yarn A purl to where Yarn B begins on previous row, change to Yarn B and K31, return to Yarn A and purl to end.

19th row Using Yarn A knit.

20th row Using Yarn A purl to 2 sts before Yarn B begins on 18th row, change to Yarn B and K35, return to Yarn A and purl to end.

21st to 24th rows Using Yarn A, beg with a knit row work 4 rows st-st.

25th row Using Yarn A K28(31:34), change to Yarn B and K1, (fur st 1, K1) 3 times, (fur st 1, K2) 5 times, return to Yarn A and knit to end.

26th row Using Yarn A purl to 3 sts before Yarn B begins on previous row, change to Yarn B and K28, return to Yarn A and purl to end.

27th row Using Yarn A knit.

28th row Using Yarn A purl to 3 sts before Yarn B begins on previous row, change to Yarn B and K33, return to Yarn A and purl to end.

29th and 30th rows Using Yarn A work 2 rows st-st.

31st row Using Yarn A K5(8:11), change to Yarn B and K1, (fur st 1, K1) 4 times, return to Yarn A and knit to end.

32nd row Using Yarn A P8(11:14), change to Yarn B and K32, return to Yarn A and purl to end.

Shape front neck

1st row (RS) Using Yarn A K23(25:27), cast off 23(25:27) sts for centre front neck, knit to end. Turn and work on this second set of 23(25:27) sts for right side of front neck. Leave first set 23(25:27) sts on a holder for left side of front neck.

2nd row (WS) Using Yarn B knit.

3rd row Using Yarn A cast off 4(5:6) sts, knit to end. 19(20:21) sts.

4th row Using Yarn B knit to end, dec 1 st at neck edge. 18(19:20) sts.

5th row Using Yarn A knit to end dec 1 st at neck edge. 17(18:19) sts.

6th row Using Yarn A purl to end, dec 1 st at neck edge. 16(17:18) sts.

7th row Using Yarn A K4(5:6), change to Yarn B, K1 (fur st 1, K1) twice, change to Yarn A and knit to end.

8th row Using Yarn A purl, dec 1 st at neck edge. 15(16:17) sts.

9th row Using Yarn A knit.

10th row Using Yarn B knit, dec 1 st at neck edge. 14(15:16) sts.

Break Yarn B.

Using Yarn A cont in st-st until armhole measures 18(19:20)cm/7(7½:8)in to shoulder shaping, ending with a RS row.

Shape shoulder

Cast off 4(5:6) sts at beg of next row and 5 sts at beg of foll alt row. 5(5:5) sts.

Next row (RS) Knit.
Cast off rem 5 sts.

Rejoin Yarn A to K23(25:27) sts left on a holder for left front neck. Work to match right side of front neck, reversing shaping and working Yarn B as desired.

CAP SLEEVES (Make 2)

Block each piece following the instructions on page 138 and referring to the ball band. Do not press the ruffled area.
Join shoulder seams.
With RS facing, using Yarn A and 4.5mm straight needles, pick up 38(40:42) sts evenly along armhole edge from start of armhole shaping excluding the cast-off sts, over the shoulder and to end of armhole shaping excluding the cast-off sts.
Work the cap sleeves in short rows (see page 133).
P34(36:38), turn, leaving rem unworked sts on needle.
K30(32:34), turn.
P26(28:30), turn.
K22(24:26), turn.
P18(20:22), turn.
K14(16:18), turn.
P10(12:14), turn.
K6(8:10), turn.
P10(12:14), working back across sts left on needle, turn.
K14(16:18), turn.
P18(20:22), turn.
K22(24:26), turn.
P26(28:30), turn.
K30(32:34), turn.
Purl back across all 38(40:42) sts.

Transfer these 38(40:42) sts onto 4.5mm double-pointed needles. Change to Yarn B and knit across the 38(40:42) sts, pick up 22 sts from underarm and join for working in the round. 60(62:64) sts.
Purl one row.
Cast off all sts.

NECKBAND

Using a 4.5mm circular needle and Yarn B cast on 4 sts. With RS of dress facing and using the needle with the cast-on sts, pick up and knit one stitch in every stitch around the neck, cast on 4 sts.
1st row Do not join in a round. Turn and knit across all stitches.
Cast off all stitches.

FINISHING

Join side and sleeve seams.
Sew the fastening button to the back of the neck. The ribbon should have sufficient gaps to allow for a button to pass through without the need to make a buttonhole.
Attach additional ribbon and buttons to the ruffled yoke if desired.

t his pretty jumper is knitted in stocking stitch in a soft silk-and-wool mix
yarn, with a fringe of shimmering nylon tape at the neck and cuffs. This
is a great way to use ribbon, tape or other fancy yarns that may not be
suitable for knitting an entire garment. Fur stitch is a good way to show off
the qualities of a more unusual yarn, such as this tape's natural drape.

'Babs' Fringed Jumper Claire Montgomerie

MATERIALS

5(6:7) 50g balls Louisa Harding Grace, shade 04 Pink. Yarn A
1(1:1) 50g ball Louisa Harding Fauve, shade 19 Beige. Yarn B
One 4.5mm (UK 7) circular needle, 80cm/31½in long
Pair 4.5mm (UK 7) knitting needles
Button to fasten, approximately 1cm/⅜in diameter

MEASUREMENTS

To fit bust

86	91	97cm
34	36	38in

Actual size

89	95	101cm
35	37½	39¾in

Length

54	57	60cm
21	22½	23½in

Sleeve seam length

26	28	30cm
10¼	11	11¾in

TENSION

21 sts and 30 rows = 10cm/4in square over stocking stitch using
Grace (Yarn A) and 4.5mm needles or the size required to obtain
the correct tension.

ABBREVIATIONS

See page 129.

fur st Fur stitch. Worked on RS rows. Knit the next stitch without
letting it drop off the LHN, bring the yarn forward between the
needles, pass the yarn around your thumb or a piece of cardboard to
make a loop approx 2cm/¾in long (or the desired length), take the
yarn back between the needles, knit the stitch on the LHN again, this
time completing it and letting it drop off the needle. Pass the first
loop of the stitch just knitted (now on the RHN) over the second loop
of the stitch just knitted and off the needle to secure stitch.

NOTES

Slip the markers when working the rounds, unless otherwise stated.

BODY

Using 4.5mm circular needle and Yarn A cast on 206(218:230) sts.
Join for knitting in the round.
1st round PM to mark beg of round, K103(109:115) sts, PM to mark
side stitch, knit to end.
2nd round Purl.
Repeating these 2 rounds forms garter stitch.
Work 4 more rounds in g-st.

7th and 8th rounds Knit.
Repeating these 2 round forms st-st.
9th round (decrease round) * Knit to st before marker, K2tog, PM;
rep from * once. 204(216:228) sts.
Cont in st-st, dec 2 sts on every foll 10th round as established to
188(200:212) sts.
Cont in st-st without shaping until work measures 36(38:40)cm/
14(15:15¾)in from cast-on edge.

FRONT

Divide for back and front

1st row Cast off 5 sts, knit to marker, place next 94(100:106) sts on
holder for the back and work on rem 89(95:101) sts
2nd row Cast off 5 sts, purl to end. 84(90:96) sts.
Cont in st-st, casting off 3 sts at beg of next 2 rows. 78(84:90) sts.
Dec 1 st at both ends of next 3 rows and on 3 foll alt rows. 66(72:78) sts.
Work 5(7:9) rows in st-st, beg and ending with a purl row.
Next row (RS) Join Yarn B and begin working the intarsia pattern,
following the chart above, starting the first stitch of the chart on the

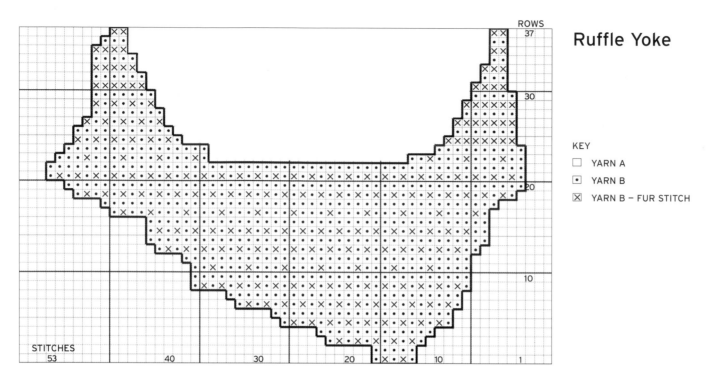

ROWS
37
30
20
10

KEY
☐ YARN A
⊡ YARN B
☒ YARN B – FUR STITCH

Ruffle Yoke

STITCHES
53   40   30   20   10   1

7th(10th:13th) stitch of the row. The first Yarn B stitch on this row is the 16th stitch of the chart [the 22nd(25th:28th) stitch of the row]. Work until armhole measures 13(14:15)cm/5(5½:6)in, ending with a WS row.

Shape neck

1st row Continuing and maintaining the intarsia pattern, K22(25:28) sts, cast off 22 sts, knit to end.
Turn and work on this second set of 22(25:28) sts for right side of front neck. Leave the first set of sts on a holder for left side of front neck.
Next row Patt.
Next row Cast off 3 sts, patt to end. 19(22:25) sts.
Dec 1 st at neck edge on next 2 rows and 4 foll alt rows 13(16:19) sts.
Cont in patt until armhole measures 18(19:20)cm/7(7½:8)in, ending with a RS row.

Shape shoulder

Cast off 4(5:5) sts at beg of next and foll alt row. 5(6:9) sts.
Cast off rem sts.

Rejoin Yarns B and A to the 22(25:28) sts left on a holder for the left side of front neck.
Work to match right side of front neck, reversing shaping.

BACK

Rejoin Yarn A to the 94(100:106) sts on the holder.
Cont in st-st, cast off 5 sts at beg of next 2 rows, and 3 sts at beg of foll 2 rows. 78(84:90) sts.
Dec 1 st at both ends of next 3 rows and 3 foll alt rows 66(72:78) sts.
Cont in st-st without shaping until armhole measures 8(9:10)cm/3(3½:4)in, ending with a WS row.

Shape neck

Next row K31(34:37), cast off 4 sts, K30(33:36). Turn and work on this second set of 31(34:37) sts for left back neck. Leave first set of sts on a holder for right side of back neck.
Cast off 1 st at neck edge on next 4 alt rows. 27(30:33) sts.
Cont in st-st without shaping until armhole measures 14(15:16)cm/5½(6:6¼)in, ending with a WS row.
Inc 1 st at neck edge on the next row, foll 4th row, then on 4 foll alt rows. 33(36:39) sts.
Cont in st-st without shaping until armhole measures 14(15:16)cm/7(7½:8)in, ending with a RS row.

Shape shoulder

Cast off 4(5:5) sts at beg of next row and foll alt row. 25(26:29) sts.
Next row (RS) Cast off 16(17:18) sts, knit to end. 9(9:11) sts.
Purl one row.
Cast off 4(4:5) sts at beg of next row, knit to end. 5(5:6) sts.
Cast off rem sts.

Rejoin Yarn A to 31(34:37) sts left on a holder for the right side of back neck.
Work to match left side of back neck, reversing shaping.

SLEEVES

Using 4.5mm circular needle and Yarn B cast on 52(54:56) sts.

1st row K1, * fur st 1, K1; rep from * to last st, K1.

2nd row Knit.

3rd row K2, * fur st 1, K1; rep from * to end.

Break Yarn B

Join Yarn A.

4th row Purl.

Work 4 more rows in st-st, ending with a WS row.

Cont in st-st, inc 1 st at both ends of next row and every foll 12th row to 62(66:68) sts. Cont in st-st without shaping until sleeve measures 26(28:30)cm/10¼(11:11¾)in from cast-on edge.

Shape sleeve top

Cast off 5 sts at beg of next 2 rows. 52(56:58) sts.

Cast off 3 sts at beg of foll 2 rows. 46(50:52) sts.

Dec 1 st at both ends of next 3 rows and 2 foll alt rows 36(40:42) sts.

Work 3(3:5) rows.

Dec 1 at both ends of next row and 4 foll 4th rows. 26(30:32) sts.

Work 1(3:5) rows.

Dec 1 st at both ends of next row and foll alt row, then on every row until 18(20:22) sts rem, ending with a WS row.

Cast off 3 sts at beg of next 4 rows. 6(8:10) sts.

Cast off rem 6(8:10) sts.

FINISHING

Block each piece following the instructions on page 138 and referring to the ball band.

Join shoulder seams and sew in sleeves.

Join side and sleeve seams.

NECK EDGING

Using a 4.5mm circular needle and Yarn A cast on 4 sts. With RS of jumper facing and using the needle with the cast-on sts, pick up 20(21:22) sts along left back neck, 14(15:16) sts along left front neck, 22 sts from cast-off edge of front neck, 14(15:16) sts along right front neck, 20(21:22) sts from right back neck, cast on 4 sts. 98(102:106) sts.

Work 2 rows g-st.

Next row (buttonhole row) K2, yo, K2tog, knit to end.

Knit one row.

Cast off knitways (on WS).

Sew on button to correspond with buttonhole.

this simple silky-knit tunic dress with wide butterfly sleeves is actually much easier to knit than it looks and can be made as long or as short as you wish, to wear on its own or over jeans. We love the Missoni-esque pattern of graduating chevron stripes, and the wonderful choice of yarns makes it slinky and shimmery, draping in all the right places.

'Mae' Tunic Dress   Louisa Harding

MATERIALS
4(4:5:5) 50g balls Louisa Harding Glisten, shade 2 Silver. Yarn A
3(3:4:4) 50g balls Louisa Harding Impression, shade 10 Blue. Yarn B
1(2:2:2) 25g balls Louisa Harding Kashmir Aran Pure, shade 6 Teal. Yarn C
2(2:3:3) 50g balls Louisa Harding Grace, shade 8 Purple. Yarn D
2(3:3:4) 50g balls Louisa Harding Impression, shade 11 Slate. Yarn E
3(3:4:4) 50g balls Louisa Harding Grace, shade 3 Dove. Yarn F
Pair each 4mm (UK 8) and 4.5mm (UK 7) knitting needles
Row counter

MEASUREMENTS
To fit bust

76 81	86-91	97-102	107-112cm
30-32	34-36	38-40	42-44in

Actual size

92	104	114	126cm
36	41	45	49½in

Finished length

81.5	81.5	81.5	81.5cm
32	32	32	32in

Sleeve seam length

30.5	30.5	30.5	30.5cm
12	12	12	12in

TENSION
23 sts and 26 rows = 10cm/4in square measured over chevron pattern using 4.5mm needles or the size required to obtain the correct tension.

ABBREVIATIONS
See page 129.

BACK AND FRONT (Make 2)
Using 4.5mm needles and Yarn A cast on 138(155:172:189) sts.

1st row (Edging 1st row) (decrease row) (RS) K1, [K2tog, K13, K2tog tbl] 8(9:10:11) times, K1. 122(137:152:167) sts.
2nd row (Edging 2nd row) (WS) Knit.
Break Yarn A.

Join Yarn B.
3rd row (Edging 3rd row) (decrease row) (RS) K1, [K2tog, K11, K2tog tbl] 8(9:10:11) times, K1. 106(119:132:145) sts.
4th row (Edging 4th row) (WS) Knit.
Break Yarn B.

Join Yarn C.
5th row (Chevron Edging 1st row) (RS) K1, [K2tog, K4, M1, K1, M1, K4, K2tog tbl] 8(9:10:11) times, K1. 106(119:132:145) sts.
6th row (Chevron Edging 2nd row) (WS) Knit.
Repeating these 2 rows forms chevron edging pattern.

7th to 12th rows Work chevron edging pattern in stripe sequence as follows:
2 rows Yarn D,
2 rows Yarn B,
2 rows Yarn E.
Break Yarn E.

Join Yarn F.
13th row (Chevron 1st row) (RS) K1, [K2tog, K4, M1, K1, M1, K4, K2tog tbl] 8(9:10:11) times, K1. 106(119:132:145) sts.
14th row (Chevron 2nd row) (WS) K1, P to last st, K1.
Repeating these 2 rows forms chevron pattern.

Continue in chevron pattern following the written instructions as follows or following the stripe sequence from the chart on page 48, starting at the 15th row until the 200th row is completed or work measures 77cm/30in, ending with a WS row.

Stripe Sequence

KEY

☐	A	▪	D
◉	B	✕	E
▪	C	·	F

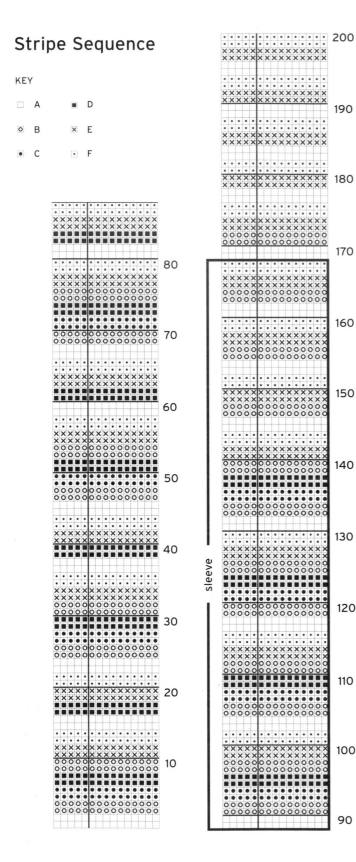

sleeve

15th to 34th rows Work chevron pattern in stripe sequence
as follows:
2 rows Yarn A,
2 rows Yarn D,
2 rows Yarn E.
21st and 22nd rows 2 rows Yarn F,
2 rows Yarn A,
2 rows Yarn B,
2 rows Yarn C,
2 rows Yarn D,
2 rows Yarn B,
2 rows Yarn E.

35th to 100th rows Repeat 13th to 34th rows 3 times.
101st to 142nd rows Repeat 21st to 34th rows 3 times.
143rd to 150th rows Work chevron pattern in stripe sequence
as follows:
2 rows Yarn F,
2 rows Yarn A,
2 rows Yarn B,
2 rows Yarn E.
151st to 174th rows Repeat 143rd to 150th rows 3 times.
175th to 180th rows Work chevron pattern in stripe sequence
as follows:
2 rows Yarn F,
2 rows Yarn A,
2 rows Yarn E.
181st to 198th rows Repeat 175th to 180th rows 3 times.
199th to 200th rows Work chevron pattern in Yarn F.
Work should measure 77cm/30in. If necessary, continue to work in
chevron pattern and stripe sequence until work measures
77cm/30in, ending with a WS row.
Break yarn.

Neck edging
Join Yarn A.
Next row (decrease row) (RS) K1, [K2tog, K9, K2tog tbl] 8(9:10:11)
times, K1. 90(101:112:123) sts.
Next row (WS) Purl.

Change to 4mm needles and work 11 rows in garter st in the following
stripe sequence:
2 rows Yarn D,
2 rows Yarn E,
2 rows Yarn F,
2 rows Yarn A,

2 rows Yarn D.

1 row Yarn B.

Using Yarn B, cast off knitways on WS.

SLEEVES (Make 2)

Using 4.5mm needles and Yarn A cast on 121 sts.

1st row (Edging 1st row) (decrease row) (RS) K1, (K2tog, K13, K2tog tbl) 7 times, K1. 107 sts.

2nd row (Edging 2nd row) (WS) Knit.

Break Yarn A.

Join Yarn B.

3rd row (Edging 3rd row) (decrease row) (RS) K1, (K2tog, K11, K2tog tbl) 7 times, K1. 93 sts.

4th row (Edging 4th row) (WS) Knit.

Break Yarn B

Join Yarn C.

5th row (Chevron Edging 1st row) (RS) K1, (K2tog, K4, M1, K1, M1, K4, K2tog tbl) 7 times, K1. 93 sts.

6th row (Chevron Edging 2nd row) (WS) Knit.

Repeating these 2 rows forms chevron edging pattern.

7th to 10th rows Work chevron edging pattern in stripe sequence as follows:

2 rows Yarn D,

2 rows Yarn B

Break Yarn B.

Join Yarn E.

11th row (Chevron 1st row) (RS) K1, [K2tog, K4, M1, K1, M1, K4, K2tog tbl] 7 times, K1. 93 sts.

12th row (Chevron 2nd row (WS) K1, P to last st, K1.

These 2 rows form the chevron pattern.

Cont in chevron pattern following the stripe sequence as for the front and back, starting at the 101st row and working until sleeve measures 30cm/12in, ending with a WS row.

Join Yarn A.

Next row (decrease row) (RS) K1, [K2tog, K9, K2tog tbl] 7 times, K1. 79 sts.

Next row K1, P to last st, K1.

Next row Knit

Cast off knitways on WS.

FINISHING

Block each piece following the instructions on page 138 and referring to the ball band.

Join shoulder seams, leaving 27cm/10½in open for the neck.

Place markers along the side edges of the front and back 20.5cm/8in on either side of shoulder seam.

Place centre of cast off edge of sleeves to shoulder seams, then sew sleeves to back and front between markers.

Join side and sleeve seams.

the wide neckline of this romantic lace-stitch chevron top has a pretty
picot cast-off and a sweet flower closure that make it ultra-feminine. The
fit around the body is relaxed and slouchy, while the wide sleeves are pulled
in tight with deep ribbed cuffs. The subtle shades of cream, butter and rose
give this gorgeous garment a sense of timeless elegance.

'Edith' Chevron Top   Louisa Harding

MATERIALS
4(4:5:5) 50g balls Louisa Harding Grace, shade 2 Soft Gold. Yarn A
2(2:2:2) 50g balls Louisa Harding Impression, shade 12 Vanilla. Yarn B
2(3:3:3) 50g balls Louisa Harding Kimono Ribbon Pure, shade 1 Rice.
  Yarn C
3(3:3:4) 50g balls Louisa Harding Grace, shade 4 Rose. Yarn D
1(2:2:3) 50g balls Louisa Harding Glisten, shade 23 Crème. Yarn E
Pair each 3.75mm (UK 9), 4mm (UK 8) and 4.5mm (UK 7) knitting
  needles

MEASUREMENTS
To fit bust

76-81	86-91	97-102	107-112cm
30-32	34-36	38-40	42-44in

Actual size

96	107	119	130cm
38	42	47	51in

Finished length

51	53.5	56	58.5cm
20	21	22	23in

Sleeve seam length

33	33	33	33cm
13	13	13	13in

TENSION
24 sts and 24 rows = 10cm/4in square measured over lace chevron
pattern using 4.5mm needles or the size required to obtain the
correct tension.

ABBREVIATIONS
See page 129.

BACK AND FRONT (Make 2)
Using 4.5mm needles and Yarn A cast on 115(129:143:157) sts.

Edging 1st row (RS) K1, K2tog, [K5, yo, K1, yo, K5, sl1, K2tog, psso]
7(8:9:10) times, K5, yo, K1, yo, K5, skpo, K1.
Edging 2nd row Knit.
These two rows form the edging pattern.
Work 4 more rows in patt.
Break Yarn A.

Join Yarn B.
Lace Chevron 1st row (RS) K1, K2tog, [K5, yo, K1, yo, K5, sl1, K2tog,
psso] 7(8:9:10) times, K5, yo, K1, yo, K5, skpo, K1.
Lace Chevron 2nd row K1, P to last st, K1.
Repeating 1st and 2nd rows forms the lace chevron pattern.
Break Yarn B.

Join Yarn C and work 2 rows lace chevron pattern.

Continue to work in lace chevron patt working 20 row stripe patt
as follows:
2 rows Yarn A,
2 rows Yarn D,
2 rows Yarn A,
2 rows Yarn C,
2 rows Yarn B,
2 rows Yarn D,
2 rows Yarn E,
2 rows Yarn D,
2 rows Yarn B,
2 rows Yarn C.

Cont in lace chevron patt and stripe sequence until work measures
47(49.5:52:54.5)cm/18½(19½:20½:21½)in ending with a WS row.
Break yarn.

Join Yarn A and work top edging.

Next row (decrease row) (RS) K1, K2tog, [K11, sl1, K2tog, psso] 7(8.9.10) times, K11, skpo, K1. 99(111.123.135) sts.
Next row K1, P to last st, K1.
Break Yarn A.

Change to 4mm needles, join Yarn D and work 2 rows in garter st.
Change to Yarn A and work 2 rows in g-st.
Change to Yarn C and work 3 rows in g-st.
Next row (WS) K1, P1, * yo, P2tog; rep from * to last st, K1.
99(111.123.135) sts.
Work 2 rows in g-st.
Change to Yarn B and work 2 rows in g-st.
Change to Yarn D and work 2 rows in g-st.
Change to Yarn E and knit 1 row.

Using Yarn E cast off 21(27.33.39) sts, then work picot cast-off as follows [slip st on RHN back onto LHN, cast on 2 sts, then cast off 5 sts] 19 times, then cast off to end.

SLEEVES (Make 2)
Using 3.75mm needles and Yarn A cast on 80 sts.
1st row (RS) * K1, P1; rep from * to end.
2nd row (WS) * K1, P1; rep from * to end.
Repeating 1st and 2nd rows forms rib.
Cont in rib until sleeve measures 13cm/5in from cast-on edge, ending with a RS row.
Next row (increase row) (WS) [Rib 4, M1, rib 3, M1] 10 times, rib 4, M1, rib 6. 101 sts.

Change to 4.5mm needles.
Next row (RS) Knit
Next row K1, purl to last st, K1.
Break Yarn A.

Join Yarn B.
Lace Chevron 1st row (RS) K1, K2tog, [K5, yo, K1, yo, K5, sl1, K2tog, psso] 6 times, K5, yo, K1, yo, K5, skpo, K1.
Lace Chevron 2nd row K1, P to last st, K1.

Repeating 1st and 2nd rows forms the lace chevron pattern.
Break Yarn B.

Join Yarn C and work 2 rows lace chevron patt.
Continue to work in lace chevron patt working 20 row stripe patt as follows:
2 rows Yarn A,
2 rows Yarn D,
2 rows Yarn A,
2 rows Yarn C,
2 rows Yarn B,
2 rows Yarn D,
2 rows Yarn E,
2 rows Yarn D,
2 rows Yarn B,
2 rows Yarn C.
Cont in lace chevron patt and stripe sequence until sleeve measures 33cm/13in from cast-on edge, ending with a WS row.
Break yarn.

Join Yarn A.
Next row (decrease row) (RS) K1, K2tog, [K11, sl1, K2tog, psso] 6 times, K11, skpo, K1. 87 sts.
Next row K1, P to last st, K1.
Next row Knit.
Cast off knitways on WS.

FINISHING
Block each piece following the instructions on page 138 and referring to the ball band.
Join shoulder seams, leaving the picot edge cast-off open for the neck.
Place markers along side edges of front and back 21cm/8½in on either side of shoulder seams.
Place centre of cast-off edge of sleeves to shoulder seams, then sew sleeves to back and front between markers.
Join side and sleeve seams.
Starting at right back shoulder edge, thread two strands of Yarn C through eyelets in top edging of back and secure in place.
Starting at right front shoulder edge, thread two strands of Yarn C through eyelets in top edging of front and secure in place.

SMALL FLOWERS (Make 3)
Using 4.5mm needles and Yarn C cast on 36 sts.
1st row * K1, cast off 4 sts (2 sts on RHN), rep from * to end. 12 sts.
Thread yarn through rem sts, pull tight and secure.
Arrange flowers on shoulder edging where ribbons meet at start of left front neck opening and sew in place using photograph as a guide.
Secure lengths of Yarn C at base of flowers to hang down like ribbons.
Cut lengths at a slanted angle to prevent fraying.
If desired, embroider French knots (see page 137) in the centre of each flower using Yarn C, and after securing let the tails hang down as ribbons.

divine
accessories

fairy-like billows of Rowan Kidsilk Haze are fashioned into a feather-light wrap or scarf using three lace patterns – knot stitch, crossed eyelet stitch and a swirl border. Perfect for an intermediate knitter who wants to try lacework, this delicate web-like design works up quickly and uses only a few balls of luxurious yarn, though it can be made to any length or width as desired.

'Anisette' Wrap

Kristeen Griffin-Grimes for French Girl

MATERIALS
1(2) 50g balls Rowan Kidsilk Haze, shade 590 Pearl
Pair 6mm (UK 4) knitting needles
One 5.5mm (UK 5) circular needle (sharp-pointed for lacework), 60cm/24in long
Stitch markers
Row counter

MEASUREMENTS
Scarf approximately 28cm/11in wide, length adjustable

Wrap approximately 76 x 142cm/30 x 60in blocked

TENSION
12 sts and 16 rows = 7.5 x 8.75cm/3 x 3½in over unblocked knot-stitch pattern using a 5.5mm circular needle or the size required to obtain the correct tension.

ABBREVIATIONS
See page 129.
C4B Place RHN needle in front of first 2 sts on LHN, insert RHN into front of next 2 sts on LHN from right to left. Slide all 4 sts off LHN, keeping original 2 sts on RHN and slipping first 2 sts off LHN. Place the loose 2 sts back on LHN, then replace the pair of sts from RHN, thereby crossing them over the sts already on LHN. Knit these 4 sts.

NOTES
The first set of figures refers to the scarf while the figures in parentheses ( ) refer to the wrap. Where only one figure is given, this applies to both the scarf and the wrap.

The number of stitches changes over the rows.

Slip the markers when working across the rows.

KNOT-STITCH SAMPLE SWATCH
Cast on a multiple of 3 sts (12 sts are used for this sample swatch).
1st row (RS) Knit.
2nd row K2, * yo, K3, then use the tip of LHN to lift the first knit stitch of the 3 sts just worked over the last two knit sts; rep from * to last st, K1.
3rd row Knit.

4th row K1, * K3, then use the tip of LHN to lift the first knit stitch of the 3 sts just worked over the last two knit sts, yo; rep from * to last 2 sts, K2. These four rows form the knot-stitch pattern

SCARF AND WRAP

Using 6mm needles and the cable method (see pages 133-4), cast on 13 sts for swirl border, PM, 12(60) sts for centre panel of scarf (wrap), PM, 13 sts for swirl border. 38(86) sts for scarf (wrap).

Change to 5.5mm circular needle and work back and forth.
1st row (RS) Sl1P, K1, yo, K2tog, yo, K5, yo, K4, SM, K12(60), SM, K4, yo, K5, yo, K2tog, yo, K2. 42(90) sts.
2nd row (WS) Sl1P, K1, purl to marker, SM, K2, * yo, K3, then use the tip of LHN to lift the first knit st of the 3 sts just worked over the last 2 knit sts; rep from * to last st before marker, K1, SM, purl to last 2 sts, K2.
3rd row Sl1P, [K2tog, yo] twice, K2, sl1, K2tog, psso, K5, SM, knit to marker, SM, K5, sl1, K2tog, psso, K2, [yo, K2tog] twice, K1. 38(86) sts.
4th row Sl1P, K1, purl to marker, SM, K1, * K3, then use the tip of LHN to lift the first knit stitch of the 3 sts just worked over the last two knit sts, yo; rep from * to last 2 sts before marker, K2, SM, purl to last 2 sts, K2.
5th row Sl1P, [K2tog, yo] twice, K2, skpo, K4, SM, knit to marker, SM, K4, skpo, K2, [yo, K2tog] twice, K1. 36(84) sts.
6th, 10th, 14th, 18th, 22nd and 26th rows Repeat 2nd row.
7th row Sl1P, [K2tog, yo] twice, K2, skpo, K3, SM, knit to marker, SM, K3, skpo, K2, [yo, K2tog] twice, K1. 34(82) sts.
8th, 12th, 16th, 20th and 24th rows Repeat 4th row.
9th row Sl1P, [K2tog, yo] twice, K2, skpo, K2, SM, knit to marker, SM, K2, skpo, K2, [yo, K2tog] twice, K1. 32(80) sts.
11th row Sl1P, K1, yo, K2tog, yo, K1, yo, K2, skpo, K1, SM, knit to marker, SM, K1, skpo, K2, yo, K1, yo, K2tog, yo, K2. 34(82) sts.
13th row Sl1P, K1, yo, K2tog, [yo, K3] twice, K1, SM, knit to marker, SM, K1, [K3, yo] twice, K2tog, yo, K2. 38(86) sts.
15th row Repeat 1st row.
17th row Repeat 3rd row.
19th row Repeat 5th row.
21st row Repeat 7th row.
23rd row Repeat 9th row.
25th row Repeat 11th row.
27th row Repeat 13th row.

FOR THE SCARF ONLY

28th row Repeat 14th row.
Continue repeating 1st to 28th rows until desired length is reached, ending with a 14th row or a 28th row. Using 6mm needles cast off loosely as given for the wrap.

FOR THE WRAP ONLY

Change to crossed eyelet stitch.
28th row and every foll alt row (WS) Sl1P, K1, purl to marker, SM, * K1, P8, K1; repeat from * 5 times, SM, purl to last 2 sts, K2.
29th row (RS) Sl1P, K1, yo, K2tog, yo, K5, yo, K4, SM, * P1, K8, P1, repeat from * 5 times, SM, K4, yo, K5, yo, K2tog, yo, K2. 90 sts.
31st row Sl1P, [K2tog, yo] twice, K2, sl1, K2tog, psso, K5, SM, * P1, K1, [skpo, yo] 3 times, K1, P1, repeat from * 5 times, SM, K5, sl1, K2tog, psso, K2, [yo, K2tog] twice, K1. 86 sts.
33rd row Sl1P, [K2tog, yo] twice, K2, skpo, K4, SM, * P1, K1, [skpo, yo] 3 times, K1, P1, repeat from * 5 times, SM, K4, skpo, K2, [yo, K2tog] twice, K1. 84 sts.
35th row Sl1P, [K2tog, yo] twice, K2, skpo, K3, SM, * P1, [skpo, yo] 3 times, K2, P1, repeat from * 5 times, SM, K3, skpo, K2, [yo, K2tog] twice, K1. 82 sts.
37th row Sl1P, [K2tog, yo] twice, K2, skpo, K2, SM, * P1, K1, [skpo, yo] twice, K3, P1, repeat from * 5 times, SM, K2, skpo, K2, [yo, K2tog] twice, K1. 80 sts.
39th row Sl1P, K1, yo, K2tog, yo, K1, yo, K2, skpo, K1, SM, P1, C4B, K4, P1, repeat from * 5 times, SM, K1, skpo, K2, yo, K1, yo, K2tog, yo, K2. 82 sts.
41st row Sl1P, K1, yo, K2tog, [yo, K3] twice, K1, SM, * P1, K8, P1, repeat from * to next marker, SM, K1, [K3, yo] twice, K2tog, yo, K2. 86 sts.
42nd row (WS) Repeat 28th row.

Repeat 29th to 42nd rows until wrap reaches desired length minus approximately 18cm/7in for remaining knot stitch, ending last repeat after a 41st row. The wrap in the photograph has 18 repeats of the crossed-eyelet-stitch pattern and the 279th row has been completed.

Change to knot stitch.
280th row (WS) Repeat 28th row.
281st row (RS) Sl1P, K1, yo, K2tog, yo, K5, yo, K4, SM, * P1, K8, P1; repeat from * to next marker, SM, K4, yo, K5, yo, K2tog, yo, K2.

282nd to 307th rows Repeat 2nd to 27th rows.
308th row Repeat 4th row.

Cast off loosely on RS as follows:
Using 6mm needles * K2tog loosely, slip the stitch just made on RHN back to LHN; repeat from *.

FINISHING
Weave in ends.
Block by the damp-finishing method (see page 138).

'Leigh's Night Out' Bag   Leigh Radford

MATERIALS

Three 100g balls Leigh Radford/Lantern Moon Silk Gelato, shade
   Melon. Yarn A

One 100g ball Leigh Radford/Lantern Moon Silk Gelato, shade Grape.
   Yarn B

Three 50g skeins Muench Yarns Touch Me, shade 3635. Yarn C

Pair 20mm knitting needles

Set 15mm double-pointed needles or circular needle, 40cm/16in long

Purse frame, 25cm/10in snap/spring frame with loops

35cm/³⁄₈yd of fabric for lining

Tapestry needle and sewing needle and thread

1m/1yd of contrasting ribbon, 5cm/2in wide (optional)

One 7.5cm/3in buckle (optional)

MEASUREMENTS

Width approximately 25cm/10in

Length approximately 25cm/10in

TENSION

6 sts (one pattern repeat) = approx 7.5-8cm/3-3½in and 8 rows
(one pattern repeat) = approx 6.5cm/2½in measured over two-tone
lattice pattern on 20mm needles or the size required to obtain the
correct tension.

ABBREVIATIONS

See Page 129.

NOTES

Colour A One strand of Silk Gelato (Melon) (Yarn A) and 2 strands
of Muench Yarns Touch Me (Yarn C) held together.

Colour B One strand of Silk Gelato (Grape) (Yarn B).

BACK AND FRONT (Make 2)

Using 20mm needles and Colour A cast on 28 sts.

1st row (WS) Knit.

Do not break Colour A.

Join Colour B.

2nd row (RS) Using Colour B K2, sl1wyib, * K4, sl2wyib; rep from *
to last 7 sts, K4, sl1wyib, K2.

3rd row (WS) Using Colour B P2, sl1wyif, * P4, sl2wyif; rep from *
to last 7 sts, P4, sl1wyif, P2.

4th row Using Colour A K2, sl1wyib, * K4, sl2wyib; rep from * to last
7 sts, K4, sl1wyib, K2.

5th row Using Colour A K2, sl1wyif, * K4, sl2wyif; rep from * to last
7 sts, K4, sl1wyif, K2.

6th row Using Colour B K4, * sl2wyib, K4; rep from * to end.

7th row Using Colour B P4, * sl2wyif, P4; rep from * to end.

8th row Using Colour A K4, * sl2wyib, K4; rep from * to end.

9th row Using Colour A K4, * sl2wyif, K4; rep from * to end.

Repeat 2nd to 9th rows once and then repeat 2nd to 8th rows.

Break Colour B.

Join Colour A.

Work 4 rows in stocking stitch beg with a purl row.

Cast off.

HANDLE

Using 15mm double-pointed needles (or circular needle) and Colour A
cast on 3 sts.

Work an I-cord 53cm/21in long (see pages 136-7).

Cast off leaving a 13cm/5in tail.

FINISHING

Join side and bottom seams with Yarn A or Yarn B.

Cut the lining fabric into a rectangle measuring 30 x 61cm/12 x 24in.
With right sides facing, fold in half lengthways so the piece measures
30 x 30cm/12 x 12in. Beginning approx 5cm/2in from the top, stitch
1-2cm/½in seams on both sides. Fold top edge of fabric over
0.5-1cm/¼ in and press. Slip lining through spring frame and fold
fabric over frame 4-5cm/1¾in with wrong sides facing each other.
Sew facing to body of lining with blind (invisible) stitch on WS. The
fabric may be slightly wider than frame; if so, gather fabric slightly
around snap/spring frame. Insert completed lining into knitted bag
with WS of lining facing WS of bag and pin in place. Sew lining into
interior of knitted bag approx 0.5-1cm/¼in below the top edge.

Attach handle by threading tail from I-cord handle into tapestry
needle and thread through loop of purse frame. Pull I-cord through
loop and secure by threading tail through centre of I-cord. Cut a
13cm/5in length of Yarn A or Yarn B and wrap at handle base as
follows: Form a loop where I-cord is threaded through metal loop of
purse frame and hold in place. Beginning approx 4-5cm/1½-2in up
from loop, wrap Yarn A or Yarn B around I-cord working back towards
loop. Thread the end through the loop and pull tight. Repeat for
opposite end of handle.

Sew ribbon and buckle to outside of bag as shown.

made in Leigh Radford's Silk Gelato yarn – Vietnamese silk cut into strips – this lush bag is perfect for that girlie boho look. Line it with crushed velvet or vintage fabric and source a great buckle or brooch as the finishing touch.

What a great way to use the divine 'Magic Balls' from Be Sweet yarns. With the simplest of patterns you have a great shawl, wrap, throw or scarf. The pattern is easy to adjust depending on what you fancy – you can make it longer or wider for a wrap or throw, narrower for a long skinny scarf, or shorter for a neck warmer; or you can add more rows of the slubby yarn.

Sweetheart Shawl   Nadine Curtis with Bardet Wardell

MATERIALS
One 50g ball Be Sweet Slubby Mohair, shade Natural. Yarn A
Two 50g balls Be Sweet Magic Balls, shade Wild Berries. Yarn B
Pair 10mm (UK 000) knitting needles

MEASUREMENTS
Length approximately 92cm/36in
Width approximately 42cm/16½in

TENSION
9 sts and 16 rows (8 ridges) = 10cm/4in square measured over garter stitch using 10mm needles or the size required to obtain the correct tension.

ABBREVIATIONS
See page 129.

NOTES
When using Yarn B, secure the knots when the ribbon ties are reached.

SHAWL
Using 10mm needles and Yarn A cast on 38 sts loosely.
1st row (WS) Knit, leaving large loops.
Break Yarn A.

Change to Yarn B.
2nd row (RS) Knit.
3rd row (WS) Knit.
Repeat 2nd and 3rd rows until both balls of Yarn B have been worked, ending with a WS row. If both balls of Yarn B look similar, reverse wind the second ball so the shawl can be somewhat symmetrical.

Change to Yarn A.
Next row Knit loosely.

Cast off knitways loosely, letting large loops remain.

FINISHING
Weave in ends.

VARIATION
The shawl can be made longer by using 3 balls of Yarn B and working the ends exactly the same.

this lace-stitch shawl in colours inspired by a 'cameo' brooch is the height of divine knitting. The drape and the attention to detail will make you feel gorgeous as soon as you put it on. The flower corsage closure, dripping with ribbons and buttons, makes it even more exquisite.

'Cameo' Shawl   Louisa Harding

MATERIALS

2(2:3:3) 50g hanks Louisa Harding Sari Ribbon, shade 7 Shell. Yarn A
2(3:3:4) 50g balls Louisa Harding Glisten, shade 4, Gold. Yarn B
4(4:5:5) 50g balls Louisa Harding Grace, shade 2 Soft Gold. Yarn C
Pair of 5mm (UK 6) knitting needles
Row counter
13 assorted mother-of-pearl buttons, approx 1-2cm/³⁄₈-³⁄₄in diameter

MEASUREMENTS

To fit bust

76-81	86-91	97-102	107-112cm
30-32	34-36	38-40	42-44in

Shoulder width

84	90	96	102cm
33	35½	38	40¼in

Width (at widest)

98	105	112	119cm
38½	41¼	44	47in

Length (without hanging ribbons)

35.5	35.5	35.5	35.5cm
14	14	14	14in

TENSION

18 sts and 28 rows = 10cm/4in square measured over lace pattern
using 5mm needles or the size required to obtain the correct tension.

ABBREVIATIONS

See page 129.

NOTES

When joining a new shade leave a tail of approx 10cm/4in for fringe
around lower edge of wrap.

When short row shaping, refer to the wrapping technique on page 133.

The number of stitches changes over the rows.

SHAWL

Using 5mm needles and Yarn A cast on 57 sts.
Work 2 rows in garter stitch.
Break Yarn A.
Join Yarn B.
Work 2 rows in g-st.

Break Yarn B.
Join Yarn C.
Work in lace and stripe pattern as follows:
1st row (RS) K10, K2tog, yo, K35, K2tog, yo, K8.
2nd row K6, K2tog, yo, K2, P33, K2tog, yo, K2, P8, K2.
3rd row K2, yo, [K2tog tbl, yo] twice, K4, K2tog, yo, K3, [yo, K2, K3tog,
K2, yo, K1] 4 times, K2tog, yo, K8. 58 sts.
4th row K6, K2tog, yo, K2, P33, K2tog, yo, K2, P9, K2. 58 sts.
5th row K2, yo, K2, [K2tog tbl, yo] twice, K3, K2tog, yo, K3, [K1, yo, K1,
K3tog, K1, yo, K2] 4 times, K2tog, yo, K8. 59 sts.
6th row K6, K2tog, yo, K2, P33, K2tog, yo, K2, P10, K2. 59 sts.
7th row K2, yo, K4, [K2tog tbl, yo] twice, K2, K2tog, yo, K3, [K2, yo,
K3tog, yo, K3] 4 times, K2tog, yo, K8. 60 sts.
8th row K6, K2tog, yo, K2, P33, K2tog, yo, K2, P11, K2. 60 sts.
9th row K1, K2tog, yo, K2tog tbl, K1, [K2tog, yo] twice, K3, K2tog, yo,
K3, [yo, K2, K3tog, K2, yo, K1] 4 times, K2tog, yo, K8. 59 sts.
10th row K6, K2tog, yo, K2, P33, K2tog, yo, K2, P10, K2. 59 sts.
11th row K1, K2tog, yo, K3tog, yo, K2tog, yo, K4, K2tog, yo, K3, [K1, yo,
K1, K3tog, K1, yo, K2] 4 times, K2tog, yo, K8. 58 sts.
12th row K6, K2tog, yo, K2, P33, K2tog, yo, K2, P9, K2. 58 sts.
13th row K1, K2tog, yo, K3tog, yo, K5, K2tog, yo, K3, [K2, yo, K3tog,
yo, K3] 4 times, K2tog, yo, K8. 57 sts.
14th row K6, K2tog, yo, K2, P33, K2tog, yo, K2, P8, K2. 57 sts.
Break Yarn C.
Join Yarn B.
15th row K10, K2tog, yo, K35, K2tog, yo, K8. 57 sts.
16th row K6, K2tog, yo, K35, K2tog, yo, K12. 57 sts.
Break Yarn B.
Join Yarn A.
17th row K10, K2tog, yo, K35, K2tog, yo, K8. 57 sts.
18th row K6, K2tog, yo, K35, K2tog, yo, K12. 57 sts.
Break Yarn A.
Join Yarn B.
19th row K10, K2tog, yo, K35, K2tog, yo, K8. 57 sts.
20th row K6, K2tog, yo, K35, K2tog, yo, K12. 57 sts.
1st to 20th rows form the lace and stripe pattern repeat.
Repeat 1st to 20th rows 12(13:14:15) times then work 1st to 14th
rows once.
Break Yarn C.
Join Yarn B.
Work 2 rows g-st
Break Yarn B.
Join Yarn A.

Work 4 rows g-st.
Cast off using Yarn A.

FINISHING
Block the shawl following the instructions on page 138 and referring to the ball bands.

Shoulder edging
With RS of shawl facing and starting at cast-off edge using 5mm needles and Yarn A pick up and knit 145(155:165:175) sts along straight edge of knitted piece.
Next row (WS) Knit.
Break Yarn A.
Join Yarn B.
1st row (RS) * K1, sl1wyib; rep from * to last st, K1.
2nd row * K1, yf, sl1wyif, yb; rep from * to last st, K1.
Join Yarn C.
3rd row Knit.
4th row Knit.
Change to Yarn B.
5th row K1, * K1, sl1wyib; rep from * to last 2 sts, K2.
6th row K1, * K1, yf, sl1wyif, yb; rep from * to last 2 sts, K2.
Break Yarn B.
Change to Yarn C.
7th row Knit.
8th row Knit.
Working in Yarn C only repeat 1st to 8th rows once then 1st to 4th rows once.
Join Yarn B.
21st row K1, * K1, sl1wyib; rep from * to last 2 sts, K2.
22nd row K1, * K1, yf, sl1wyif, yb; rep from * to last 2 sts, K2.
Change to Yarn C.
23rd row Knit.
24th row Knit.
Break Yarn C.
Change to Yarn B.
25th row * K1, sl1wyib; rep from * to last st, K1.
26th row * K1, yf, sl1wyif, yb; rep from * to last st, K1.
Break Yarn B.
Join Yarn A.
27th row Knit.
Cast off knitways on WS decreasing across row as follows:
Cast off 1, [K2tog, cast off, cast off 8], 14(15:16:17) times, cast off rem st.

Button edging
With RS of shawl facing and using 5mm needles and Yarn A pick up and knit 12 sts along left front edge of shoulder edging.
Cast off knitways on WS.

Button loop edging
With RS of shawl facing and using 5mm needles and Yarn A pick up and knit 12 sts along right front edge of shoulder edging.
Next row (Button loop row) (WS) K1 (one stitch on RHN), * insert LHN from front to back into stitch on RHN and knit it; rep from * until a chain of 5 sts has been made. Then pick up first chain stitch made with LHN, knit this stitch again and then take last chain stitch made over this stitch (button loop made), cast off 3 sts (one stitch on RHN). Rep from * 3 times.
Sew buttons on left front to correspond with button loops.

Flower corsage
Two-colour rosette (Make 2)
Using 5mm needles and Yarn A cast on 112 sts leaving a long tail.
Break Yarn A, leaving a long tail.
Join Yarn C.
1st row Knit.
2nd row K2, [K1, slip this st back onto LHN, lift the next 8 sts on LHN over this st and off needle, knit the first st again, K2] 10 times. 32 sts.
3rd row Knit 24 sts, turn.
4th row Knit to end.
5th row Knit 16 sts, turn.
6th row Knit to end.
7th row Knit 8 sts, turn.
8th row Knit to end.
Cut yarn and thread through stitches on needle, pull tightly to create a rosette and secure with a few stitches. Do not sew in or trim Yarn A tails.

Small flowers (Make 7)
Using 5mm needles and Yarn B cast on 36 sts.
1st row * K1, cast off 4 sts (2 sts on needle); rep from * to end. 12 sts.
Cut yarn and thread yarn through sts on needle, pull tight and secure with a few stitches.

Arrange flowers on shoulder edging and sew in place using photograph as a guide.
Sew a button in the centre of each flower.
Secure all lengths of yarn at lower edge of wrap and at the beginning and end of the first row of the rosettes to hang down like ribbons.
Cut all lengths of ribbons at a slanted angle to prevent them from fraying.

he knitted bobbles embellished with sparkling beads and the lushness and texture of the bouclé mohair in soft peach and grey makes this the prettiest and cosiest neck warmer around.

Bouclé Neck Warmer   Juju Vail

MATERIALS

One 50g ball Be Sweet Bouclé Mohair, shade Peach. Yarn A
One 50g ball Be Sweet Bouclé Mohair, shade Dark Grey. Yarn B
One 50g ball Louisa Harding Grace, shade 3. Yarn C
Pair each 5mm (UK 6) and 7mm (UK 2) knitting needles
One 8mm (UK 0) knitting needle
16 crystal rose montee beads or other 4mm crystals
Fibrefill or other stuffing for bobbles
Beading needle and thread

MEASUREMENTS

Length without cords and bobbles 62cm/24½in
Length with cords and bobbles approximately 120cm/47in
Width approximately 18cm/7in

TENSION

22 sts and 34 rows = 10cm/4in square over stocking stitch using Yarn C on 5mm needles or the size required to obtain the correct tension.
13 sts and 26 rows (13 ridges) = 10cm/4in square over garter stitch using Yarn A on 7mm needles or the size required to obtain the correct tension.

ABBREVIATIONS

See page 129.

FIRST BOBBLE

Using 5mm needles and Yarn C cast on 8 sts.
1st row (RS) Knit.
2nd row Purl.
3rd row (K1, M1) 8 times. 16 sts.
4th row Purl.
5th row * K1, M1, K2; rep from * to last st, K1, M1. 22 sts.
Work 7 rows st-st, beg and ending with a purl row.
13th row * K2tog, K2; rep from * to last 2 sts, K2tog. 16 sts.
14th row Purl.
15th row (K2tog) 8 times. 8 sts.
16th row Purl.
17th row Knit.

18th row (WS) Purl.
Do not cast off. Break Yarn C.

FIRST CORD

Join Yarn B.
1st row (RS) K2tog, knit to end. 7 sts.
2nd row P2tog, purl to end. 6 sts.
Cont in st-st until cord measures 25cm/10in, ending with a purl row.
Do not cast off. Break Yarn B.

NECK WRAP

Change to 7mm needles and join Yarn A.
1st row (RS) (K1, M1) 6 times. 12 sts.
2nd row Knit.
3rd row (K1, M1, K2) 4 times. 16 sts.
4th row Knit.
5th row K2, (K1, M1, K3) 3 times, K1, M1, K1. 20 sts.
6th row Knit.
Cont in garter stitch without shaping until the neck wrap measures 60cm/24in from the start of Yarn A, ending with a WS row.

Next row (RS) K2, (K2tog, K3) 3 times, K2tog, K1. 16 sts.
Next row Knit.
Next row (K2tog, K2) 4 times. 12 sts.
Next row Knit.
Next row (K2tog) 6 times. 6 sts.
Next row (WS) Knit.
Do not cast off. Break Yarn A.

SECOND CORD

Change to 5mm needles and join Yarn B.
1st row (RS) Knit.
2nd row Purl.
Cont in st-st until cord measures 25cm/10in, ending with a purl row.
Next row (RS) K1, M1, knit to end. 7 sts.
2nd row P1, M1, purl to end. 8 sts.
Do not cast off. Break Yarn B.

SECOND BOBBLE

Change to 5mm needles and Yarn C. Make
the second bobble following the instructions
for the first bobble, starting at the 1st row.
When complete, break yarn leaving a long
tail. Thread the tail through all the stitches
on the needle and pull to close.

FINISHING

Block the wrap following the instructions
on page 138 and referring to the ball bands.
Join bobble seam to within 1cm/½in of top.
Add stuffing until the bobble is a nice round
shape then complete the seam.
Join cord seam using Yarn B to the beginning
of neck wrap section.
Repeat for the other bobble and cord.
Sew 8 crystal beads around the middle circumference
of each bobble.

FRILL

Using 7mm needles and Yarn B, with RS facing pick
up 70 stitches along one edge of neck wrap section.
1st row (WS) Purl.
2nd row (K1, M1) 70 times. 140 sts
3rd row Purl.
Cast off using an 8mm needle.
Repeat frill on opposite edge.
Weave in ends of frill to meet the grey cord.

these pretty corsages are extremely versatile - wear them on a lapel, hat, bag or any other garment or accessory you wish to brighten up. Pile up two or three to create a bouquet of gorgeous knitted ruffles or wear them singly; there's also the option of adding more or fewer layers or 'petals'. The patterns are straightforward and quick to make; it doesn't matter if they knit up smaller or larger than the pattern suggests, so any yarn can be used. In fact, oddments from your stash are an ideal place to start.

Flower Corsages   Claire Montgomerie

MATERIALS
One 50g ball Debbie Bliss Alpaca Silk, shade 23 Bright Turquoise. Yarn A
One 50g ball Be Sweet Ribbon, shade Silver. Yarn B
One 50g ball ggh Bel Air, shade 21 Lime. Yarn C
One 50g ball Rowan Pure Wool DK, shade 042 Vivid Purple. Yarn D
One 50g ball Be Sweet Ribbon, shade Plum. Yarn E
One 50g ball Alchemy Synchronicity, shade Silver. Yarn F
One 50g ball Louisa Harding Fauve, shade 6 Lime. Yarn G
One 50g ball Rooster Almerino Aran, shade 303 Strawberry Cream. Yarn H
One 50g ball ggh Soft Kid, shade 55 Pale Pink. Yarn I
Pair each 4mm (UK 8) and 6.5mm (UK 3) knitting needles or the size appropriate for the yarn you decide to use
2 pairs 5.5mm (UK 5) knitting needles or the size appropriate for the yarn you decide to use
Large brooch backs, safety pins or kilt pins
Sewing needle and thread

MEASUREMENTS
Diameter at the widest point:
Corsage One 16cm/6½in
Corsage Two 14cm5½in
Corsage Three 18cm/7in

TENSION
The correct tension is not a requirement.

ABBREVIATIONS
See page 129.
Fur st Fur stitch. Worked on RS rows. Knit the next stitch without letting it drop off LHN, bring the yarn forward between the needles, pass the yarn around your thumb or a piece of cardboard to make

Opposite: See page 92 for Cable Wrap pattern.

a loop approx 2cm/¾in long (or the desired length), take the yarn back between the needles, knit the stitch on the LHN again, this time completing it and letting it drop off the needle. Pass the first loop of the stitch just knitted (now on RHN) over the second loop of the stitch just knitted and off the needle to secure stitch.

CORSAGE ONE (CIRCULAR SHAPE)

First circle

Using 6.5mm needles and Yarn A cast on 88 sts.

Break Yarn A.

Join Yarn B.

1st and 2nd rows Knit.

3rd row * K9, K2tog; rep from * to end. 80 sts.

4th row Knit.

5th row * K8, K2tog; rep from * to end. 72 sts.

6th row Knit.

7th row * K7, K2tog; rep from * to end. 64 sts.

8th row Knit.

9th row * K6, K2tog; rep from * to end. 56 sts.

10th row Knit.

11th row * K5, K2tog; rep from * to end. 48 sts.

12th row Knit.

13th row * K4, K2tog; rep from * to end. 40 sts

14th row Knit.

15th row * K3, K2tog; rep from * to end. 32 sts.

16th row Knit.

17th row * K2, K2tog; rep from * to end. 24 sts.

18th row Knit.

19th row * K1, K2tog; rep from * to end. 16 sts.

20th row Knit.

21st row * K2tog; rep from * to end. 8 sts.

Cut yarn leaving approx 30cm/12in tail, thread through rem stitches and pull up tight to draw into a circle. Join seam to complete circle.

Second circle

Using 6.5mm needles and Yarn C cast on 80 sts.

1st and 2nd rows Knit.

Work as for first circle from 5th row onwards.

Third circle

Using 6.5mm needles and Yarn D cast on 72 sts.

Break Yarn D.

Opposite: You can use as many layers as you wish: the small corsage (top) is made up of the fourth and fifth circles of Corsage One, shown in its entirety below.

Join Yarn E.

1st row Knit.

Work as for first circle from 7th row onwards.

Fourth circle

Using 4mm needles and Yarn F cast on 64 sts.

1st row Knit.

2nd row Purl.

Work as for first circle from 9th row onwards, but working even rows as purl instead of knit, thus working in stocking stitch. When joining the seam, allow the cast-on edge to roll to the RS, as is natural with st-st.

Fifth circle

Using 6.5mm needles and Yarn G cast on 30 sts.

1st row Knit.

2nd row K1, * fur st 1; rep from * to last st, K1.

3rd row Knit.

Cut yarn leaving approx 30cm/12in tail. Thread yarn through rem stitches and pull, making strip curl in on itself. Sew in place in centre of fourth circle as a curled rosette.

FINISHING

Layer the circles on top of one another, largest at the bottom to smallest at the top, and sew in place.

Make as many layers as desired, leaving out or adding in layers as you wish.

Attach the brooch back or pin to the back of the corsage, towards the top centre to prevent the layers from drooping.

CORSAGE TWO (FLOWER SHAPE)

First layer – strip one

Using 6.5mm needles and Yarn E cast on 90 sts.

1st row Purl.

2nd row K2, * K1 and slip this st back onto LHN, with the tip of RHN, lift next 8 sts after the first st, one at a time, over and off LHN, yo2, knit first st on LHN again, K2; rep from * to end.

3rd row Knit, drop first yo of previous row, work [K1, K1 tbl, K1] into second yo. 50 sts.

Place all stitches on a holder.

First layer – strip two

Using 6.5mm needles and Yarn H cast on 106 sts.

1st and 2nd rows Purl.

3rd row K2, * K1 and slip this st back onto LHN, with the tip of RHN, lift next 10 sts after the first st, one at a time, over and off LHN, yo2, knit first st on LHN again, K2; rep from * to end.

4th row K1 * P2tog, drop first yo of previous row, [K1, P1, K1, P1] into second yo, P1; rep from * to last st, K1. 50 sts.

5th row Knit.

Place all sts on a holder.

First layer – strip three

Using 6.5mm needles and Yarn E cast on 114 sts.

1st to 3rd rows Purl.

4th row K2, * K1 and slip this st back onto LHN, with the tip of RHN, lift next 11 sts after the first st, one at a time, over and off LHN, yo2, knit the first st on LHN again, K2; rep from * to end.

5th row K1 * P2tog, drop first yo of previous row, [K1, P1, K1, P1] into second yo, P1; rep from * to last st, K1. 50sts.

6th row Knit.

7th row Knit, while at the same time joining the second strip of petals. Hold the needle containing the stitches from Strip Three and the stitch holder containing the stitches from Strip Two together in your left hand. WS of Strip Two should be against RS of Strip Three. Insert RHN knitways into the first stitch on the front needle and then insert the tip of RHN into the first stitch on the back needle and knit these two stitches together onto RHN.

8th row Knit.

9th row Knit, while at the same time joining the first strip of petals as described on the 7th row.

10th row * K2tog, K3; rep from * to end. 40 sts.

11th row Knit.

12th row * K2tog, K2; rep from * to end. 30 sts.

13th row Knit.

CORSAGE THREE (PETAL SHAPE)

First layer – strip one

Using 5.5mm needles and Yarn F cast on 5 sts.

1st row (WS) P1, M1, purl to last st, M1, P1. 7 sts.

2nd row K1, M1, knit to last st, M1, K1. 9 sts.

3rd, 5th and 7th rows Purl.

4th row K1, M1, knit to last st, M1, K1. 11 sts.

6th row K1, M1, knit to last st, M1, K1. 13 sts.

8th row K1, M1, knit to last st, M1, K1. 15 sts.

Work 5 rows st-st, beg and ending with a purl row.

14th row K5, skpo, K1, K2tog, K5. 13 sts.

15th, 17th, 19th and 21st rows Purl.

16th row K4, skpo, K1, K2tog, K4. 11 sts.

18th row K3, skpo, K1, K2tog, K3. 9 sts.

20th row K2, skpo, K2tog, K2. 7 sts.

22nd row K1, skpo, K1, K2tog, K1. 5 sts.

23rd row Purl.

Leave this petal on the needle. Make 5 more, leaving each on the needle next to the last. Alternatively, the petals can be left on a stitch holder.

Above: Flower-shaped Corsage Two (complete).
Right: The centres of the corsages can be worn on their own, without the surrounding petals, as shown on page 70. This is the centre of Corsage Three.

14th row * K2tog, K1; rep from * to end. 20 sts.

15th row Knit.

16th row *K2tog; rep from * to end. 10 sts.

Cut yarn leaving approx 30cm/12in tail, thread through rem stitches and pull up tight to draw into a circle. Join seam to complete circle.

Second layer

Using 6.5mm needles and holding Yarns D, F, G and I together cast on 3 sts.

Work 10cm/4in garter stitch.

Cast off first stitch and fasten off second stitch. Let the last stitch unravel back down to cast-on edge.

Roll up the strip into a circle, with loops on top, and sew in place.

FINISHING

Lay the second layer on top of the first, in the centre of the petals, and sew in place.

Attach the brooch back or pin to the back of the corsage, towards the top centre to prevent the layers from drooping.

First layer – strip two

Using 5.5mm needles and Yarn C cast on 5 sts.

1st row (WS) Purl.

2nd row K1, M1, knit to last st, M1, K1. 7 sts.

3rd and 5th rows Purl.

4th row K1, M1, knit to last st, M1, K1. 9 sts.

6th row K1, M1, knit to last st, M1, K1. 11 sts.

Work 5 rows st-st, beg and ending with a purl row.

12th row K3, skpo, K1, K2tog, K3. 9 sts.

13th and 15th rows Purl.

14th row K2, skpo, K1, K2tog, K2. 7 sts.

16th row K1, skpo, K1, K2tog, K1. 5 sts.

17th row Purl.

Leave this petal on the needle. Make 7 more, leaving each on the needle next to the last. Alternatively, the petals can be left on a stitch holder.

First layer – strip three

Using 5.5mm needles and Yarn H cast on 3 sts.

1st, 3rd and 5th rows (WS) Purl.

2nd row K1, M1, knit to last st, M1, K1. 5 sts.

4th row K1, M1, knit to last st, M1, K1. 7 sts.

6th row K1, M1, knit to last st, M1, K1. 9 sts.

Work 5 rows st-st, beg and ending with a purl row.

12th row K2, skpo, K1, K2tog, K2. 7 sts.

13th row Purl.
14th row K1, skpo, K1, K2tog, K1. 5 sts.
15th row Purl.
Leave this petal on the needle. Make 7 more, leaving each on the needle next to the last. Alternatively, the petals can be left on a stitch holder. Do not break off Yarn H.

Assemble all petals in order, with RS facing for the next row, with the first petal made at the knob end of LHN and the last petal made at the tip of LHN.
Continuing in Yarn H, knit first 4 stitches of last petal made, knit together last stitch of petal and first stitch of next. Continue in this way, knitting together the last and first stitches of each petal until the last six, largest petals, are reached. Knit along these, joining them, yet not knitting together the stitches of adjoining petals, but just knitting along the 5 stitches of each petal normally. 95 sts.
Work 4 rows garter stitch on these 95 sts.
Cast off knitways.

Second layer

Using 6.5mm needles and Yarn B cast on 64 sts.
1st to 3rd rows Knit.
Work as for first circle of Corsage One from the 9th row, and sew up accordingly.

Right: Petal-shaped Corsage Three (complete).

Third layer

Using 6.5mm needles and Yarn I cast on 4 sts.
Work in garter stitch for approx 20cm/8in.
Cast off first st and fasten off second stitch. Let the last 2 stitches unravel back down to cast-on edge.

Fourth layer

Using 6.5mm needles and Yarns A, G and I held together cast on 20 sts.
1st row K1, * fur st 1; rep from * to last st, K1.
Cut yarn leaving approx 30cm/12in tail, thread yarn through rem stitches and pull up, making strip roll into a rosette. Secure in place.

FINISHING

Lay out the first layer in a rosette, with largest leaves on the bottom, spiralling up to the small pink petals, and sew in place. If the yarn used is fairly soft, the leaves may need to be secured with a few stitches so they don't flop down when worn.
Lay the second layer on top and sew in place.
Lay the last two layers in the centre of the second layer, with the third layer wrapped around the fourth layer, and secure.
Attach the brooch back or pin to the back of the corsage, towards the top centre to prevent the layers from drooping.

no girl can have too many bags and this pretty turquoise one is ideal for knitting, shopping or work. The rows of bobbly raspberry stitch and threaded ribbon elevate the simple rectangular shape into the loveliest bag. Line it with fabric you love and find great Perspex, wood or bamboo handles.

Raspberry-Stitch Bag   Kate Samphier

MATERIALS

Eight 50g balls Frog Tree Chunky Alpaca, shade 61
Pair 5mm (UK 6) knitting needles
Pair bag handles (these have a straight opening 29cm/11½in wide)
50cm/18in of lining fabric, and matching sewing thread and needle
Two 1m/1yd lengths of cream ribbon, 3cm/1¼in wide
Two 50cm/20in lengths of cream ribbon, 3cm/1¼in wide

MEASUREMENTS

Width approximately 39cm/15½in
Length without handles approximately 35cm/14in

TENSION

20 stitches and 24 rows = 10cm/4in square measured over stocking stitch using 5mm needles or the size required to obtain the correct tension.

ABBREVIATIONS

See page 129.

BAG

Using 5mm needles cast on 83 sts.
Work 12 rows in stocking stitch beginning with a knit row.

Ribbon eyelet panel

** 1st row (RS) Knit.
2nd and 4th rows Knit.
3rd row * K2tog tbl, yo; rep from * to last st, K1.

Stocking-stitch panel

Work 8 rows st-st, inc 1 st at end of last row. 84 sts.

Raspberry-stitch panel

1st row (RS) Purl.
2nd row * (K1, P1, K1) into next stitch, P3tog; rep from * to end.
3rd row Purl.

4th row * P3tog, (K1, P1, K1) into next stitch; rep from * to end.
Repeat 1st to 4th rows 4 times.
Next row (RS) Purl, dec 1 st at end of row. 83 sts.

Stocking-stitch panel

Beg and ending with a purl (WS) row, work 7 rows st-st. **
Rep from ** to ** 4 times.

Ribbon eyelet panel

1st row (RS) Knit.
2nd and 4th rows Knit.
3rd row * K2tog tbl, yo; rep from * to last st, K1.
Beg with a knit row work 12 rows st-st.
Cast off.

FINISHING

Block following instructions on page 138 and referring to the ball band.
Cut lining fabric to size of knitted piece plus a seam allowance of 1-2cm/¼-½in all round. PM at each side edge of knitted piece halfway along first raspberry-stitch panel from cast-on edge. Repeat for cast-off edge. PM at corresponding points on lining fabric.
Fold knitting in half, WS facing, so cast-on edge meets cast-off edge and central eyelet panel is at fold. Join side seams between bottom of bag and markers.
Thread 50cm/20in lengths of ribbon through the eyelets closest to cast-on and cast-off edges and secure ends.
Fold lining in half widthways and join side seams to the markers. Fold over the unsewn length of side edge to WS of lining and press.
With WS of lining facing WS of bag, insert lining into bag.
Insert cast-on edge of bag through one handle, from RS to WS, and fold over stocking stitch on WS, with ribbon eyelet panel remaining on RS. Stitch cast-on edge in place. Repeat for cast-off edge.
Fold over top of lining to WS and sew in place to cover cast-on and cast-off edges. Sew lining in place at side edges.
Thread a 1m/1yd length of ribbon through the eyelets across the centre of each side of the bag. Knot ends of ribbon together.

bell-shaped flowers dangle on their stems from the moss-stitch bow of this quirky brooch. For a variation add beads in the centres or alternate flowers with baby pompoms. You could also make a cluster of flowers and hang them on a crocheted string to make a necklace.

Bell-Flower Brooch   Julie Arkell

MATERIALS

One 50g ball ggh Bel Air in each of five shades: 1 Light Pink, 3 Deep
  Plum, 5 Bright Pink, 9 Burnt Orange and 21 Mustard for the flowers,
  bobbles and bows. Yarn A
One 50g ball ggh Bel Air, shade 19 Green for the stems. Yarn B
Pair 3.25mm (UK 10) knitting needles
Two 3.25mm (UK 10) double-pointed knitting needles
Tapestry needle
Large safety pin or brooch pin

MEASUREMENTS

Brooch approximately 10 x 15cm/4 x 6in
Bell flower finished length without bobble approximately 5cm/2in

TENSION

The correct tension is not a requirement.

ABBREVIATIONS

See page 129.

NOTE

The flowers, bobbles and bows are made in assorted colours of the
knitter's choice (Yarn A).

BELL FLOWER (Make 5 in different colours)

Using 3.25mm needles and Yarn A cast on 15 sts.
Beg with a knit row, work 8 rows in stocking stitch.
9th row * K3, K2tog; rep from * to end. 12 sts.
10th, 12th and 14th rows Purl.
11th row * K2, K2tog; rep from * to end. 9 sts.
13th row * K2, K2tog; rep from * once, K1. 7 sts.
15th row * K1, K2tog; rep from * once, K1. 5 sts.
16th row Purl.
Cut yarn leaving a tail approx 20cm/8in long. Thread tail through
remaining stitches, gather the stitches and leave.

STEM (Make 5)

Using 3.25mm double pointed needles and Yarn B cast on 3 sts.
Work an I-cord 10cm/4in long (see page 136-7).
Cast off.

BOBBLES (Make 5 in different colours)

Using 3.25mm needles and Yarn A cast on I stitch, leaving a long tail.

1st row (WS) [K1 into the front and K1 into the back of the stitch]
3 times. 6 sts.
2nd and 4th rows (RS) Purl.
3rd and 5th rows Knit.
6th row [P2tog] 3 times. 3 sts.
7th row Sl1, K2tog, psso. 1 st.
Fasten off, leaving a long tail.
To form the bobble, thread one of the tails through a tapestry needle
and work a running stitch around the shape. Pull the thread firmly
to form a bobble, leaving the other tail hanging free – this will go
through the bell flower.

BOW (Make 1)

Using 3.25mm needles and Yarn A cast on 7 sts.
1st row K1, * P1, K1; rep from * to end.
Repeating 1st row forms moss stitch.
Work 27 more rows in moss st.
Cast off in moss stitch.

BOW CENTRE (Make 1)

Using 3.25mm needles and Yarn A cast on 5 sts.
Work 12 rows in moss st as for the bow.
Cast off in moss stitch.

FINISHING

Find middle of bow and work running stitch up the centre,
gathering slightly.
Take centre piece of bow and sew the top edge onto back of bow,
about 5mm/¼in from bow edge. Repeat at the bottom.
Thread the tapestry needle with the tail at the top of a bell flower.
Choose a contrasting bobble to hang down the centre, making sure
it can be seen below bottom opening of flower.
Pass the long tail of the bobble through the top of the flower and
then pull the top of the flower tight to secure. Then sew a seam at
the back of the flower to form bell shape.
Turn up cast-on edge a little so the reverse stocking stitch of bell
flower can be seen.
Sew in cast-off tails on stems. With the cast on tail sew a stem to
a bell flower.
When all five flowers are completed gather them together, with
seams at the back, so they hang unevenly.
Sew stems to the back of bow
Sew a large safety pin or brooch pin onto back of bow.

this pattern can be adapted in many different ways. In addition to this version, a necklace may be composed of many small bows strung together, just one large one, or any combination of sizes you wish; it is also possible to attach a single bow to a pin to wear as a brooch. The bows can be knitted in any yarn using up odd balls from a stash. This silk has been chosen for its weight, drape and sheen, making the bows hang as prettily as jewels.

Bow Necklace   Claire Montgomerie

MATERIALS
One 50g ball Debbie Bliss Pure Silk, shade 009 Lilac. Yarn A
One 50g ball Debbie Bliss Pure Silk, shade 003 Cream. Yarn B
Pair 4mm (UK8) knitting needles or size appropriate for the yarn used
One 3mm (UK 11) crochet hook
Button to fasten, approximately 6-8mm/¼-⅜ inch diameter

MEASUREMENTS
Length from top of bow to end of tie
Large bow approximately 20cm/8in
Small bow approximately 8cm/3¼in

TENSION
The correct tension is not a requirement.

LARGE BOW (Make 1)
Using 4mm needles and Yarn A cast on 9 sts.
1st row K1, * P1, K1; rep from * to end.
Repeating 1st row forms moss stitch.
Cont in moss stitch until strip measures 62cm/24½in.
Cast off in moss stitch.

Bow centre
Using 4mm needles and Yarn B cast on 7 sts.
Work in moss stitch as for the bow until strip measures 6cm/2½in.
Cast off in moss stitch.

Fold the long strip into a bow shape, crossing the ends over at the back. Fasten by wrapping the short strip around the middle where the bow folds over itself. Sew the ends of the short strip together at the back to finish and secure with a few stitches through the bow centre if desired.

SMALL BOW (Make 2)
Using 4mm needles and Yarn B cast on 5 sts.
Work in moss stitch as for the large bow until strip measures 30cm/12in.
Cast off in moss stitch.

Bow centre
Using 4mm needles and Yarn B cast on 5 sts.
Work in moss stitch as for the large bow until strip measures 4cm/1½in.
Cast off in moss stitch.

Make the small bow as for the large bow.

NECKLACE
Using a 3mm crochet hook and Yarn B make a length of chain 15cm/6in long or desired length. Make a second chain 3cm/1¼in longer than the first, then make a loop at the end by working 1 slip st into the chain 3cm/1¼in from hook.
Sew the button onto one end of the shorter chain and use the loop on the second chain as a buttonhole to fasten.

FINISHING
Sew one small bow to each side of the large bow, joining the folded parts. Sew one chain to each small bow at the centre back. Weave in all ends.

beautiful boudoirs

avender is renowned for its soothing, sleep-inducing properties and this
sweet lavender-filled pillow makes a cosy decoration for a bed while
giving off a calming and relaxing aroma. The dusky pink wool cover is
knitted in a mixture of diamond pattern and bird cable stripe, creating
a textural design that is offset by the luxe velvet ribbon.

Lavender Sleep Pillow   Ruth Cross

MATERIALS
Five 50g balls Rowan Little Big Wool, shade 504 Amethyst
Pair 7mm (UK 2) knitting needles
1sq m/1sq yd of cotton fabric
Several scoops of dried lavender
50cm/½yd of matching double-sided velvet ribbon, 2cm/¾in wide
Sewing needle and thread

MEASUREMENTS
Width of main piece before folding 68cm/26¾in
Width after folding 42cm/16½in
Height, top to bottom 32cm/12½in

TENSION
13 sts and 18 rows = 10cm/4in square measured over stocking stitch
on 7mm needles or the size required to obtain the correct tension.
If your tension is correct for stocking stitch, then it will be correct
for the pattern.

ABBREVIATIONS
See page 129.
Cable 6 Slip next 2 stitches onto a cable needle and hold at back
of work, K1 from LHN, K2 from cable needle, then slip next stitch
onto a cable needle and hold at front of work, K2 from LHN, K1
from cable needle.

NOTES
Refer to the special cast-on, knit and purl techniques described on
pages 31-2.

Making a buttonhole
Bring yarn to front of work, slip 1 stitch from LHN to RHN, pass yarn
between the needles to back of work and leave.
Slip another stitch from LHN to RHN, pass the first stitch over it –

1 stitch cast off. Repeat this process until 4 stitches for buttonhole have been cast off.

Slip the loop on RHN back to LHN and turn work.

Pick up hanging yarn and pass it between the needles to back of work. Now cast on 5 stitches using the cable cast-on (see page 130). Before placing last loop on LHN, bring yarn through the needles to the front forming a dividing strand between the last stitch and the next-to-last stitch. Turn work again.

Slip the first stitch from LHN to RHN, then pass the last (extra) cast-on stitch over it. Buttonhole completed. Continue working across row.

PILLOW COVER

Using 7mm needles cast on 111 stitches.

1st row (WS) Purl.

2nd row (RS) K2, sl2wyib, K2, [K1, yo, K3, K2tog, K4, yo] 3 times, K1, yo, K3, K2tog, K2, sl2wyib, K5, yo, K3, K2tog, K4, yo, K5, sl2wyib, K7, yo, [K1, yo, K3 K2tog, K4, yo] 3 times, K3, sl2wyib, K2. 119 sts.

3rd row P2, sl2wyif, P2, [P5, P2tog, P4] 3 times, P5, P2tog, P2, sl2wyif, P9, P2tog, P9, sl2wyif, P7, [P5, P2tog, P4] 3 times, P3, sl2wyif, P2. 111 sts.

4th row Cable 6, [K2, yo, K2, K2tog, K3, yo, K1] 3 times, K2, yo, K2, K2tog, cable 6, K4, yo, K2, K2tog, K3, yo, K4, cable 6, K4, yo, K1, [K2, yo, K2, K2tog, K3, yo, K1] 3 times, K1, cable 6. 119 sts.

5th row P6, [P5, P2tog, P4] 3 times, P5, P2tog, P13, P2tog, P18, [P5, P2tog, P4] 3 times, P7. 111 sts.

6th row K2, sl2wyib, K2, [K3, yo, K1, K2tog, K2, yo, K2] 3 times, K3, yo, K1, K2tog, K2, sl2wyib, K7, yo, K1, K2tog, K2, yo, K7, sl2wyib, K5, yo, K3, [K2, yo, K1, K2tog, K2, yo, K3] 3 times, K2, sl2wyib, K2. 119 sts.

7th row P2, sl2wyif, P2, [P5, P2tog, P4] 3 times, P5, P2tog, P2, sl2wyif, P9, P2tog, P9, sl2wyif, P2, P5, [P5, P2tog, P4] 3 times, P3, sl2wyif, P2. 111 sts.

8th row Cable 6, [K4, yo, K2tog, K1, yo, K3] 3 times, K4, yo, K2tog, cable 6, K6, yo, K2tog, K1, yo, K6, cable 6, K2, yo, K4, [K3, yo, K2tog, K1, yo, K4] 3 times, cable 6. 119 sts.

9th row Repeat 5th row. 111 sts.

10th row K2, sl2wyib, K7, [yo, K1, yo, K3, K2tog, K4] 3 times, yo, K3, sl2wyib, K2, yo, K1, K2tog, K4, yo, K1, yo, K3, K2tog, K2, yo, K2, sl2wyib, K3, yo, [K3, K2tog, K4, yo, K1, yo] 3 times, K3, K2tog, K2, sl2wyib, K2. 120 sts.

11th row P2, sl2wyif, P12, [P2tog, P9] twice, P2tog, P7, sl2wyif, P4, P2tog, P9, P2tog, P4, sl2wyif, P7, [P2tog, P9] 3 times, P2tog, P2, sl2wyif, P2. 111 sts.

12th row Cable 6, K4, [yo, K3, yo, K2, K2tog, K3] 3 times, yo, K2, cable 6, yo, K1, K2tog, K3, yo, K3, yo, K2, K2tog, K2, yo, cable 6, K2, [yo, K2, K2tog, K3, yo, K3] 3 times, yo, K2, K2tog, cable 6. 120 sts.

13th row P16, [P2tog, P9] twice, P2tog, P13, P2tog, P9, P2tog, P13, [P2tog, P9] 3 times, P2tog, P6. 111 sts.

14th row K2, sl2wyib, K5, [yo, K5, yo, K1, K2tog, K2] 3 times, yo, K5, sl2wyib, K2, yo, K1, K2tog, K2, yo, K5, yo, K1, K2tog, K2, yo, K2, sl2wyib, K5, [yo, K1, K2tog, K2, yo, K5] 3 times, yo, K1, K2tog, K2, sl2wyib, K2. 120 sts.

15th row Repeat 11th row. 111 sts.

16th row Cable 6, K2, [yo, K7, yo, K2tog, K1] 3 times, yo, K4, cable 6, K1, yo, K2tog, K1, yo, K7, yo, K2tog, K1, yo, K1, cable 6, K4, [yo, K2tog, K1, yo, K7] 3 times, yo, K2tog, cable 6. 120 sts.

17th row Repeat 13th row. 111 sts.

2nd to 17th rows form the pattern.

Repeat 2nd to 12th rows once.

Next row P2, make buttonhole, P10, [P2tog, P9] twice, P2tog, P13, P2tog, P9, P2tog, P13, [P2tog, P9] 3 times, P2tog, make buttonhole, P2.

Repeat 14th to 17th rows once.

Repeat 2nd to 17th rows once more.

Repeat 2nd to 11th rows once.

58 rows pattern worked in all.

Cast off knitways.

PILLOW UNDERFLAP

Using 7mm needles cast on 30 sts.

1st row (RS) Knit.

2nd row Purl.

Repeating these 2 rows forms stocking stitch.

Cont in st-st until the underflap measures the same length as the body, ending with a purl row.

Cast off knitways.

FINISHING

Fold the short sides of the cover towards the centre, right sides together so the cables on the front and back match. Pin these ends in position.

Then place the underflap centrally over the gap so the knit side is showing (the purl side will show on the outside when it's finished). Sew along the top and bottom and turn right side out.

To make the lavender pillow

Measure the folded knitted pillow cover and cut 2 pieces of matching fabric to the same size, adding a 2cm/¼in seam allowance to the length and width.

Sew 1cm/¼in in from the edge nearly all the way round and turn right side out.

Fill with lavender through the gap and neatly sew up the opening. Insert the pillow into the knitted cover and use the ribbon to draw the two sides together.

Floral Bolster Cushion Catherine Tough

MATERIALS
Three 100g balls Rowan Big Wool, shade 37 Zing. Yarn A
One 50g ball ggh Bel Air, shade 01 Light Pink. Yarn B
One 50g ball ggh Bel Air, shade 20 Olive Green. Yarn C
One 50g ball ggh Bel Air, shade 11 Brown. Yarn D
One 50g ball ggh Bel Air, shade 03 Red. Yarn E
One 50g ball ggh Bel Air, shade 19 Green. Yarn F
Pair each 5mm (UK 6) and 12mm knitting needles
Cushion pad to fit (approximately 55 x 55cm/22 x 22in folded in half)
Invisible monofilament thread or matching sewing thread and needle
Wooden button, 3.5cm/1½in diameter

MEASUREMENTS
30 x 55cm/12 x 21½in

TENSION
7½ sts and 10 rows = 10cm/4in square measured over stocking stitch using Big Wool and 12mm needles or the size required to obtain the correct tension.
16 sts and 22 rows = 10cm/4in square measured over stocking stitch before felting using Bel Air and 5mm needles or the size required to obtain the correct tension.

ABBREVIATIONS
See page 129.

NOTE
The main part of this bolster is basically a rectangle and is knit in seven alternating sections of garter and stocking stitch.

BOLSTER COVER
Using 12mm needles and Big Wool cast on 25 stitches.
Work in g-st until bolster cover measures 18cm/7in.
Beg with a knit row work in st-st for 11cm/4¼in (until bolster cover measures 29cm/11¼in), ending with a RS (knit) row.
Work in g-st for 22cm/8¾in (until bolster cover measures 51cm/20in), ending with a WS row.
Work in st-st for 27cm/10½in (until bolster cover measures 78cm/30½in), ending with a RS row.
Work in g-st for 15cm/6in (until bolster cover measures 93cm/36½in), ending with a WS row.
Work in st-st for 20cm/8in (until bolster cover measures 113cm/44½in), ending with a RS row.

Work in g-st for 3cm/1¼in (until bolster cover measures 116cm/45¾in), ending with a WS row.
Work in st-st for 2cm/¾in (until bolster cover measures 118cm/46½in), ending with a WS row.

Cast-off and buttonhole row (RS) Cast off 12 stitches then * wind the yarn round the RHN and bring it through the loop on the RHN. Repeat from * 4 times. Knit together the next two stitches on the LHN and cast off the next stitch on the RHN to make a neat finish on the button loop. Complete the cast-off to the end of the row.

PM at both ends of the centre row (59cm/23¼in from each short edge).

FLOWERS (Make 2, one in Yarn B and one in Yarn C)
Using 5mm needles and Yarn B cast on 32 sts.
Beg with a knit row work 20cm/8in st-st.
Cast off.
The piece will measure approx 20 x 20cm/8 x 8in.

Felting
The pieces are felted until they are stable enough to be cut and not fray. This can be done by hand, alternately washing in hot and cold water while rubbing with washing liquid. Alternatively, use a 40° cycle in a washing machine. (Each machine is different, so it is better to start at a lower temperature and build up the intensity of the wash until the pieces are felted as desired.) Felting will shrink the knitted pieces.

FINISHING
Block each piece following the instructions on page 138 and referring to the ball bands or gently press using a steam iron and leave until dry.
Fold the buttonhole edge of the cover to the centre row. Fold the other short edge beyond the centre row to form an underlap on the RS until the finished cover measures 55cm/21½in long. Pin in place and join the side seams.
Cut out petals and leaves from the felted pieces and place them on the cover. They can be attached temporarily with double-sided tape or pins until you are happy with the design.
Hand-stitch round the petals using an invisible or matching thread.
Embroider the stems in backstitch and embroider buds and highlights using Yarns D, E and F.
Sew on the button.
Insert the pad into the cover.

perfect on a bed, sofa, armchair or daybed, this lovely bolster cushion is knitted in garter stitch and stocking stitch, creating a gorgeous textured effect. There are charming clusters of flowers, twigs and felted leaves in contrasting colours, of which you can make more or fewer, depending on the look you are after.

m elt back into your comfort zone. There's a Danish word 'hygge', which means cosy, warm and glowing – and this sumptuous hottie cover makes you feel like that. With its chunky cream yarn knitted into rows of pretty cables and the velvet ribbon tie, it looks gorgeous on the bed any time of day and is an irresistible bed-fellow on cold nights.

Hot-Water Bottle Cover

Ruth Cross

MATERIALS
Four 100g balls Blue Sky Alpacas Bulky, shade 1004 Polar
Pair 7mm (UK 2) knitting needles
Cable needle
Row counter
1.5m/1½yds of pale pink double-sided velvet ribbon, 2cm/¾in wide

MEASUREMENTS
Cover width 24.5cm/9⅝in
Length to ribbon holes 29cm/11½in
Length above ribbon holes 8cm/3¼in
Cast-on edge width 49cm/19¼in
Length one cable repeat 4cm/1½in

TENSION
11½ sts and 13½ rows = 10cm/4in square over stitch pattern using Blue Sky Alpacas Bulky and 7mm needles or the size required to obtain the correct tension.

ABBREVIATIONS
See page 129.
C4B Slip next 2 sts onto cable needle and hold at back of work, K2 from LHN then K2 from cable needle.
C4F Slip next 2 sts onto cable needle and hold at front of work, K2 from LHN then K2 from cable needle.

HOT-WATER BOTTLE COVER
Using 7mm needles cast on 57 sts.
1st row (RS) Knit.
2nd, 4th and 6th rows P21, [yo, sl1wyif, P2tog, psso, yo, P2] twice, P1, [yo, sl1wyif, P2tog, psso, yo, P2] 5 times.
3rd and 5th rows K48, yo, sl1wyib, K2tog, psso, yo, K2, yo, sl1wyib, K2tog, psso, yo, K1.
7th row K38, C4B, C4F, K2, yo, sl1wyib, K2tog, psso, yo, K2, yo, sl1wyib, K2tog, psso, yo, K1.
Repeat 2nd to 7th rows 5 times, then repeat 2nd and 3rd rows once.

40th row (WS) P16, [yo, sl1wyif, P2tog, psso, yo, P2] 3 times, P1, [yo, sl1wyif, P2tog, psso, yo, P2] 5 times. PM at both ends of this row.
41st row K43, [yo, sl1wyib, K2tog, psso, yo, K2] twice, yo, sl1wyib, K2tog, psso, yo, K1.
Repeat 40th and 41st rows 4 times.
Cast off knitways on WS.

FINISHING
Block the cover following the instructions on page 138 and referring to the ball band.
Fold the cover in half and join the side and bottom seams.
On the 40th row, use the natural holes on either side of each twist stripe where the cable ends to thread the ribbon.

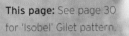

This page: See page 30 for 'Isobel' Gilet pattern.

drape this soft dusky-pink wrap around your shoulders anytime, anywhere, and it will instantly make you feel special, whether you wear it over a strappy dress on a chilly summer evening or wrapped around you while you're reading in bed or knitting. From the sweet detail of the narrow turned-down collar to the small cable twists, we love this wrap.

Cable Wrap   Debbie Bliss

MATERIALS
9(10) 50g balls of Debbie Bliss Cashmerino DK, shade 16 Pale Pink
One 4mm (UK 8) circular knitting needle, 80cm/32in long
One 3.75mm (UK 9) circular knitting needle, 80cm/32in long
Cable needle
Large kilt pin or brooch to fasten

MEASUREMENTS
To fit bust
81-92	97-107cm
32-36	38-42in

Actual size at lower edge
152	156cm
60	61½in

Length at centre back
36	39cm
14½	15½in

TENSION
22 sts and 30 rows = 10cm/4in square measured over stocking stitch using 4mm needles or the size required to obtain the correct tension.

ABBREVIATIONS
See page 129.
C4[6:8]B Slip next 2[3:4] sts onto cable needle and hold at back of work, K2[3:4] from LHN, then K2[3:4] from cable needle.
C4[6:8]F Slip next 2[3:4] sts onto cable needle and hold at front of work, K2[3:4] from LHN, then K2[3:4] from cable needle.
C4/2B Slip next 2 sts onto cable needle and hold at back of work, K2tog tbl from LHN, then K2tog from cable needle.
C4/2F Slip next 2 sts onto cable needle and hold at front of work, K2tog from LHN, then K2tog tbl from cable needle.
C6/4B Slip next 3 sts onto cable needle and hold at back of work, [K2tog tbl, K1] from LHN, then [K2tog, K1] from cable needle.

C6/4F Slip next 3 sts onto cable needle and hold at front of work, [K1, K2tog] from LHN, then [K1, K2tog tbl] from cable needle.
C8/6B Slip next 4 sts onto cable needle and hold at back of work, [K2, K2tog tbl] from LHN, then [K2tog, K2] from cable needle.
C8/6F Slip next 4 sts onto cable needle and hold at front of work, [K2, K2tog] from LHN, then [K2, K2tog tbl] from cable needle.
C10/8B [Slip next 3 sts onto cable needle and hold at back of work, K2 from LHN, then [K2tog tbl, K1] from cable needle] twice.
C10/8F [Slip next 2 sts onto cable needle and hold at front of work, [K2tog, K1] from LHN, then K2 from cable needle] twice.

NOTES
When short row shaping, refer to the wrapping technique on page 133.

RIGHT HALF
Using a 4mm circular needle cast on 221(229) sts.
1st row (WS) [K4, P4] 1(2) times, [K7, P8, K7, P4, K7, P4] 5 times, K7, P8, K7, P4, K2.
2nd row P2, [C4B, P7, C8B, P7, C4B, P7] 5 times, C4B, P7, C8B, P7, [C4B, P4] 1(2) times.
3rd, 5th and 7th rows Repeat 1st row.
4th row P2, [K4, P7, K8, P7, K4, P7] 5 times, K4, P7, K8, P7, [K4, P4] 1(2) times.
6th row P2, [C4B, P7, K8, P7, C4B, P7] 5 times, C4B, P7, K8, P7, [C4B, P4] 1(2) times.
8th row Repeat 4th row.
These 8 rows form the pattern.
Repeat 1st to 8th rows 8(9) times, then repeat the 1st row once. 73(81) rows worked in all.

Shape shoulder
1st row (RS) P2, [C4B, P7, C8B, P7, C4B, P7] 4 times, C4B, P2tog, P5, C8/6B, P5, P2tog, [C4B, P7] twice, C8B, P7, [C4B, P4] 1(2) times. 217(225) sts.

This page: See page 88 for Floral Bolster Cushion pattern.

2nd and every alternate row to 26th row (WS) P all purl sts and K all knit sts as they appear to maintain st-st cables and reverse st-st background.

3rd row P2, [K4, P7, K8, P7, K4, P7] 4 times, K4, P6, K6, P6, [K4, P7] twice, K8, P7, [K4, P4] 1(2) times.

5th row P2, [C4B, P7, K8, P7, C4B, P7] 4 times, C4B, P6, K6, P6, [C4B, P7] twice, K8, P7, [C4B, P4] 1(2) times.

7th row P2, [K4, P7, K8, P7, K4, P7] 4 times, K4, P2tog, P4, C6B, P4, P2tog, [K4, P7] twice, K8, P7, [K4, P4] 1(2) times. 215(223) sts.

9th row P2, [C4B, P7, C8B, P7, C4B, P7] 4 times, C4B, P5, K6, P5, [C4B, P7] twice, C8B, P7, [C4B, P4] 1(2) times.

11th row P2, [K4, P7, K8, P7, K4, P7] 4 times, K4, P5, K6, P5, [K4, P7] twice, K8, P7, [K4, P4] 1(2) times.

13th row P2, [C4B, P7, K8, P7, C4B, P7] 4 times, C4B, P2tog, P3, C6/4B, P3, P2tog, [C4B, P7] twice, K8, P7, [C4B, P4] 1(2) times. 211(219) sts.

15th row P2, [K4, P7, K8, P7, K4, P7] 4 times, [K4, P4] twice, [K4, P7] twice, K8, P7, [K4, P4] 1(2) times.

17th row P2, [C4B, P7, C8B, P7, C4B, P7] 4 times, C4B, P2tog, P2, C4B, P2, P2tog, [C4B, P7] twice, C8B, P7, [C4B, P4] 1(2) times. 209(217) sts.

19th row P2, [K4, P7, K8, P7, K4, P7] 4 times, [K4, P3] twice, [K4, P7] twice, K8, P7, [K4, P4] 1(2) times.

21st row P2, [C4B, P7, K8, P7, C4B, P7] 4 times, C4B, P2tog, P1, C4B, P1, P2tog, [C4B, P7] twice, K8, P7, [C4B, P4] 1(2) times. 207(215) sts.

23rd row P2, [K4, P7, K8, P7, K4, P7] 4 times, [K4, P2] twice, [K4, P7] twice, K8, P7, [K4, P4] 1(2) times.

25th row P2, [C4B, P7, C8B, P7, C4B, P7] 4 times, C4B, P2tog, C4/2B, P2tog, [C4B, P7] twice, C8B, P7, [C4B, P4] 1(2) times. 203(211) sts.

27th row P2, [K4, P7, K8, P7, K4, P7] 4 times, K3, ssk, K2, K2tog, K3, P7, K4, P7, K8, P7, [K4, P4] 1(2) times. 201(209) sts.

28th row (WS) [K4, P4] 1(2) times, K7, P8, K7, P4, K7, P10, [K7, P4, K7, P8, K7, P4] 4 times, K2.

29th row P2, [C4B, P7, K8, P7, C4B, P7] 4 times, C10/8B, P7, C4B, P7, K8, P7, [C4B, P4] 1(2) times. 199(207) sts.

30th row (WS) [K4, P4] 1(2) times, K7, P8, K7, P4, K7, P8, [K7, P4, K7, P8, K7, P4] 4 times, K2.

31st row P2, [K4, P7, K8, P7, K4, P7] 4 times, K8, P7, K4, P7, K8, P7, [K4, P4] 1(2) times.

32nd row (WS) Repeat 30th row.

33rd row P2, [C4B, P7, C8B, P7, C4B, P7] 4 times, C8B, P7, C4B, P7, C8B, P7, [C4B, P4] 1(2) times.

34th row Repeat 30th row.

35th row Cast off all sts, working [K1, K2tog, K1] across each 4-st cable and [K1, K2tog, K2, K2tog, K1] across each 8-st cable.

LEFT HALF

Using a 4mm circular needle cast on 221(229) sts.

1st row (WS) K2, [P4, K7, P8, K7, P4, K7] 5 times, P4, K7, P8, K7, [P4, K4] 1(2) times.

2nd row [P4, C4F] 1(2) times, [P7, C8F, P7, C4F, P7, C4F] 5 times, P7, C8F, P7, C4F, P2.

3rd, 5th and 7th rows Repeat 1st row.

4th row [P4, K4] 1(2) times, [P7, K8, P7, K4, P7, K4] 5 times, P7, K8, P7, K4, P2.

6th row [P4, C4F] 1(2) times, [P7, K8, P7, C4F, P7, C4F] 5 times, P7, K8, P7, C4F, P2.

8th row Repeat 4th row.

These 8 rows form the pattern.

Repeat 1st to 8th rows 8(9) times, then repeat the 1st row once. 73(81) rows worked in all.

Shape shoulder

1st row (RS) [P4, C4F] 1(2) times, P7, C8F, [P7, C4F] twice, P2tog, P5, C8/6F, P5, P2tog, C4F, [P7, C4F, P7, C8F, P7, C4F] 4 times, P2. 217(225) sts.

2nd and every alternate row to 26th row (WS) P all purl sts and K all knit sts as they appear to maintain st-st cables and reverse st-st background.

3rd row [P4, K4] 1(2) times, P7, K8, [P7, K4] twice, P6, K6, P6, K4, [P7, K4, P7, K8, P7, K4] 4 times, P2.

5th row [P4, C4F] 1(2) times, P7, K8, [P7, C4F] twice, P6, K6, P6, C4F, [P7, C4F, P7, K8, P7, C4F] 4 times, P2.

7th row [P4, K4] 1(2) times, P7, K8, [P7, K4] twice, P2tog, P4, C6F, P4, P2tog, K4, [P7, K4, P7, K8, P7, K4] 4 times, P2. 215(223) sts.

9th row [P4, C4F] 1(2) times, P7, C8F, [P7, C4F] twice, P5, K6, P5, C4F, [P7, C4F, P7, C8F, P7, C4F] 4 times, P2.

11th row [P4, K4] 1(2) times, P7, K8, [P7, K4] twice, P5, K6, P5, K4, [P7, K4, P7, K8, P7, K4] 4 times, P2.

13th row [P4, C4F] 1(2) times, P7, K8, [P7, C4F] twice, P2tog, P3, C6/4F, P3, P2tog, C4F, [P7, C4F, P7, K8, P7, C4F] 4 times, P2. 211(219) sts.

15th row [P4, K4] 1(2) times, P7, K8, [P7, K4] twice, [P4, K4] twice, [P7, K4, P7, K8, P7, K4] 4 times, P2.

17th row [P4, C4F] 1(2) times, P7, C8F, [P7, C4F] twice, P2tog, P2, C4F, P2, P2tog, C4F, [P7, C4F, P7, C8F, P7, C4F] 4 times, P4. 209(217) sts.

19th row [P4, K4] 1(2) times, P7, K8, [P7, K4] twice, [P3, K4] twice, [P7, K4, P7, K8, P7, K4] 4 times, P2.

21st row [P4, C4F] 1(2) times, P7, K8, [P7, C4F] twice, P2tog, P1, C4F, P1, P2tog, C4F, [P7, C4F, P7, K8, P7, C4F] 4 times, P2. 207(215) sts.

23rd row [P4, K4] 1(2) times, P7, K8, [P7, K4] twice, [P2, K4] twice, [P7, K4, P7, K8, P7, K4] 4 times, P2.

25th row [P4, C4F] 1(2) times, P7, C8F, [P7, C4F] twice, P2tog, C4/2F, P2tog, C4F, [P7, C4F, P7, C8F, P7, C4F] 4 times, P2. 203(211) sts.

27th row [P4, K4] 1(2) times, P7, K8, P7, K4, P7, K3, ssk, K2, K2tog, K3, [P7, K4, P7, K8, P7, K4] 4 times, P2. 201(209) sts.

28th row (WS) K2, [P4, K7, P8, K7, P4, K7] 4 times, P10, K7, P4, K7, P8, K7, [P4, K4] 1(2) times.

29th row [P4, C4F] 1(2) times, P7, K8, P7, C4F, P7, C10/8F, [P7, C4F, P7, K8, P7, C4F] 4 times, P2. 199(207) sts.

30th row (WS) K2, [P4, K7, P8, K7, P4, K7] 4 times, P8, K7, P4, K7, P8, K7, [P4, K4] 1(2) times.

31st row [P4, K4] 1(2) times, P7, K8, P7, K4, P7, K8, [P7, K4, P7, K8, P7, K4] 4 times, P2.

32nd row (WS) Repeat 30th row.

33rd row [P4, C4F] 1(2) times, P7, C8F, P7, C4F, P7, C8F, [P7, C4F, P7, C8F, P7, C4F] 4 times, P2.

34th row Repeat 30th row.

35th row Cast off all sts, working [K1, K2tog, K1] across each 4-st cable and [K1, K2tog tbl, K2, K2tog tbl, K1] across each 8-st cable.

COLLAR

Block each piece following the instructions on page 138 and referring to the ball band.

Join back seam.

With right side facing and using a 3.75mm circular needle, pick up and knit 137 sts along cast-off edge to centre of first shaped cable, then pick up and knit 65(77) sts to centre of second shaped cable, then pick up and knit 137 sts to end. 339(351) sts.

1st row (WS) Knit.

2nd row (RS) Knit to last 160(166) sts, turn.

3rd row Sl1, K20, turn.

4th row Sl1, K22, turn.

5th row Sl1, K24, turn.

6th row Sl1, K26, turn.

Cont working short rows in this way, working 2 more sts on every row until the row 'Sl1, K88, turn' has been worked.

Next row (RS) Sl1, K92, turn.

Next row Sl1, K96, turn.

Cont working short rows in this way, working 4 more sts on every row until the row 'Sl1, K128, turn' has been worked.

Next row Sl1, K136, turn.

Cont working short rows in this way, working 8 more sts on every row until the row 'Sl1, K176, turn' has been worked.

Next row Sl1, knit to end.

Next row Using a 4mm needle, cast off 90(96) sts knitways, cast off next 159(159) sts purlways, then cast off rem 90(96) sts knitways.

FINISHING

Fold the wider part of the collar over onto the right side, wrap around your shoulders with the shaped cables on your shoulders and fasten with a gorgeous brooch or large kilt pin.

b ed socks may not be the most seductive articles of clothing to wear in the boudoir, but your feet will thank you for them on chilly nights and they're great to wear around the home instead of slippers. The super-soft socks with a flirty lace ruffle are the ideal pattern to use divine pure cashmere yarn, as they require only a small quantity. There's nothing better to spoil your feet with, and you'll never want to take them off.

Lace Ruffle Bed Socks   Leslie Scanlon

MATERIALS

Two 55g skeins Jade Sapphire 6-ply DK Mongolian Cashmere, shade 65 Silver Fox
Set of 3.25mm (UK 10) double-pointed needles
Set of 3.5mm double-pointed needles
Set of 3.75mm (UK 9) double-pointed needles
Set of 4.5mm (UK 7) double-pointed needles
Stitch markers
Tapestry needle

MEASUREMENTS

Shoe/Sock size

S	M	L
4-5	6-7	8-9

Foot length

23cm/9in	24cm/9½in	15.5cm/10in

The foot length is adjustable.

TENSION

22 sts and 30 rows = 10cm/4in square measured over stocking stitch on 3.25mm needles or the size required to obtain the correct tension.

ABBREVIATIONS

See page 129.

NOTES

When making a yo after a knit stitch and before a purl stitch, bring the yarn to the front between the needles, then over the top of the RHN and back to the front (also known as yarn round needle).
When making a yo after a purl stitch and before a knit stitch, take the yarn to the back between the needles, then over the top of the RHN and between the needles to the back again.

SOCK (Make 2)

Using 3.75mm double-pointed needles cast on 40(44:48) sts evenly onto 3 needles.
Join for knitting in the round and PM at the beginning of the round.
1st round * K1, P1; rep from * to end.
Repeating this round forms K1, P1 rib.
Cont rib until sock measures 7.5(9:10)cm/3(3½:4)in.

Divide for heel and instep

Knit to the marker then K10(12:12) sts after the marker. The 10(12:12) sts before the marker and the 10(12:12) sts after the marker are the 20(24:24) sts for the heel.
Divide the rem 20(20:24) sts evenly onto 2 needles for the instep.

Using 3.25(3.25:3.5)mm double-pointed needles, work the heel sts back and forth as follows:
1st row (WS) Sl1P, purl to end.
2nd row (RS) Sl1K, * K1, sl1K; rep from * to last st, K1.
Rep 1st and 2nd rows 9(10:12) times, ending with a RS row. 20(22:24) rows worked.

Turn the heel

1st row (WS) Sl1P, P11(13:13), P2tog tbl, P1, turn.
2nd row Sl1K, K5, K2tog tbl, K1, turn.
3rd row Sl1P, purl to 1 st before previous turn, P2tog tbl, P1, turn.
4th row Sl1K, knit to 1 st before previous turn, K2tog tbl, K1, turn.
Repeat 3rd and 4th rows until all sts have been worked, ending with a 4th row and omitting the P1 at the end of the penultimate row and the K1 at the end of the last row. 12(14:14) sts.

Form the gusset

Place half of the remaining heel sts onto another 3.25(3.25:3.5)mm double-pointed needle and, using the same needle, with RS facing, pick up and knit 10(11:12) slipped sts along the side of the heel. Combine the 20(20:24) sts for the instep from the next 2 double-pointed needles onto another 3.25(3.25:3.5)mm double-pointed needle and knit these sts. With a third 3.25(3.25:3.5)mm double-pointed needle, pick up and knit 10(11:12) slipped sts along the other side of the heel. On the same double-pointed needle, knit the remaining half of the heel sts (this is now the centre back of the heel). 52(56:62) sts.

Resume knitting in the round. Join and PM at the beginning of the round.

1st round Knit.

2nd round On first needle, knit to last 3 sts, K2tog, K1; on second needle, knit all sts; on third needle K1, ssk, knit to end. Repeat 1st and 2nd rounds until 40(44:48) sts rem.

Cont working in the round without shaping until the sock measures 18.5(19.5:21)cm/7¼(7¾:8)in or 4.5cm/1¾in less than the desired length, measuring from the back of the heel to the tip of the big toe.

Shape toe

1st round On first needle, knit to last 3 sts, K2tog, K1; on second needle, K1, ssk, knit to last 2 sts, K2tog, K1; on third needle, K1, ssk, knit to end.

2nd round Knit.

Repeat 1st and 2nd rounds until 12(16:20) sts rem.

Join toe

Kitchener-stitch/graft the toe together as follows (see pages 139-40):

Small size and Large size

K3(5) sts from first needle to fourth (empty) needle and slip 3(5) sts from third needle to the other end of the fourth needle. The first and third needles are now empty. There are now 6(10) sts on both the second and fourth needles.

Medium size

K4 sts from first needle to fourth (empty) needle and slip 4 sts from third needle to the other end of the fourth needle. Slip last st on first needle to second needle and the remaining stitch on the third needle to the other end of the second needle. The first and third needles are now empty. There are now 8 sts on both the second and fourth needles.

All sizes

Holding the 2 needles parallel, with a threaded tapestry needle * go into the first st on the front needle as if to knit and pull the st off the needle, then go into the next st on the front needle as if to purl and leave this st on the needle. Now go into the first st on the back needle as if to purl and pull this st off the needle, then go into the second st on the back needle as if to knit and leave that st on the needle.

Repeat from * until 1 st remains on each needle. Weave yarn through rem sts and secure on the wrong side.

RUFFLE

With the RS facing, using 3.5mm needles and starting at the centre back of the rib, pick up 40(44:48) sts all round.

Change to 4.5mm needles and work back and forth as follows:

1st row (WS of ruffle, RS of sock) * K3, P1; rep from * to end. 40(44:48) sts.

2nd row K1, * P3, K1, rep from * to last 3 sts, P3.

3rd row K3, * yo, P1, yo, K3; rep from * to last st, P1. 58(64:70) sts.

4th row K1, * P3, K3; rep from * to last 3 sts, end P3.

5th row K3, * yo, P3, yo, K3; rep from * to last st, P1. 76(84:92) sts.

6th row K1, * P3, K5; rep from * to last 3 sts, P3.

7th row K3, * yo, P5, yo, K3; rep from * to last st, P1. 94(104:114) sts.

8th row K1, * P3, K7; rep from * to last 3 sts, P3.

9th row K1, * yo, K2tog tbl; rep from * to last st, P1. 94(104:114) sts.

10th row Knit.

Cast off.

FINISHING

Join ruffle seam.

Weave in all ends.

Block each piece following the instructions on page 138 and referring to the ball band. Or, with a pressing cloth, gently block the ruffle by spreading it out flat a small amount at a time.

this pretty floral throw will have you yearning for more lounging time. It is super-cosy as well as beautiful, and would be a welcome extra layer on the bed on chilly nights or make a great throw to snuggle under in front of the TV. You can make it as large as you like by adding on more squares, and you can play around with the configuration of the flowers and leaves, either attaching them at regular intervals on the blanket or scattering them over its surface in random clusters.

Flower Posy Throw **Nicki Trench**

MATERIALS
Sixteen 50g balls of Rowan Pure Wool DK, shade 001 Clay. Yarn A
One 50g ball Rowan Pure Wool DK, shade 025 Tea Rose. Yarn B
One 50g ball Rowan Pure Wool DK, shade 032 Gilt. Yarn C
One 50g ball Rowan Pure Wool DK, shade 019 Avocado. Yarn D
One 50g ball Rowan Pure Wool DK, shade 026 Hyacinth
One 50g ball Rowan Pure Wool DK, shade 027 Hydrangea
One 50g ball Rowan Pure Wool DK, shade 028 Raspberry
One 50g ball Rowan Pure Wool DK, shade 029 Pomegranate
Pair 4mm (UK 8) knitting needles, 35cm/14in long
One 4mm (UK 8) circular needle, 60cm/24in long (optional)
Pair 3.5mm knitting needles
Row counter

MEASUREMENTS
Length including edging approximately 135cm/53in
Width including edging approximately 105cm/41in
Each square 30 x 30cm/12 x 12in

TENSION
22 sts and 30 rows = 10cm/4in square measured over stocking stitch using Rowan Pure Wool DK on 4mm needles or the size required to obtain the correct tension.

ABBREVIATIONS
See page 129.

NOTES
For the top and bottom edgings, the stitches will fit but with a tight squeeze onto 35cm/14in-long 4mm needles. You may find it easier to use a 60cm/24in-long 4mm circular needle and work back and forth. After the flowers have been sewn in place, the seams of the throw can be hidden by working mattress stitch (see pages 138–9) up the vertical seams and working Swiss darning (cover stitch) over the horizontal seams (see page 140).

SQUARES FOR THROW (Make 12)
Using 4mm needles and Yarn A cast on 66 sts.
Beg with a knit row work 90 rows st-st.
Cast off.

Join the squares
Block each square following the instructions on page 138 and referring to the ball band.
Join squares with backstitch to make one large rectangle, 3 squares across and 4 squares down.
When joining the squares, the 3 squares at the top and the 3 squares at the bottom must have the cast-off edges at the outer edge of the throw, ready for picking up stitches for the edgings.

TOP EDGING
Using 4mm needles and Yarn A pick up and knit 193 sts evenly across the top of the throw.
1st row Sl1, * K1, P1, rep from * to end.
2nd row Sl1, M1, * K1, P1, rep from * to last 2 sts, K1, M1, K1. 195 sts.
3rd row Sl1, * P1, K1; rep from * to end.
4th row Sl1, M1, * P1, K1; rep from * to last st 2 sts, P1, M1, P1. 197 sts.
Repeating these 4 rows forms moss stitch with corner shaping.

Repeat 1st to 4th rows 6 times. 221 sts.
Cast off in moss stitch.

BOTTOM EDGING
Work as for top edging.

SIDE EDGING (Make 2)
Increasing side edging
Using 4mm needles and Yarn A cast on 2 sts.
1st row (WS) K1, P1.
2nd row Sl1, M1, K1. 3 sts.

3rd row Sl1, P1, K1.
4th row Sl1, M1, P1, K1. 4 sts.
5th row Sl1, P1, K1, P1.
6th row Sl1, M1, K1, P1, K1. 5 sts.
7th row Sl1, P1, K1, P1, K1.
8th row Sl1, M1, [P1, K1] twice. 6 sts.
9th row Sl1, P1, [K1, P1] twice.
10th row Sl1, M1, * K1, P1; rep from * to last st, K1. 7 sts.
11th row Sl1, * P1, K1; rep from * to end.
12th row Sl1, M1, * P1, K1; rep from * to end. 8 sts.
13th row Sl1, * P1, K1; rep from * to last st, P1.

Repeat 10th to 13th rows 4 times, then 10th and 11th rows once. 17 sts.

Main part of side edging

Next row Sl1, * P1, K1; rep from * to end.
Next row Sl1, * P1, K1; rep from * to end.
Repeating these 2 rows forms moss stitch.
Repeat these 2 rows for another 358 rows or until the narrower edge of the main part of the side edging, when slightly stretched, fits along the side of the throw to the cast-off edge of the 4th square, ending at the narrower edge.

Decreasing side edging

1st row Sl1, K2tog, * P1, K1; rep from * to end. 16 sts.
2nd row Sl1, * P1, K1; rep from * to last st, P1.
3rd row Sl1, P2tog, * K1, P1; rep from * to last st, K1. 15 sts.
4th row Sl1, * P1, K1; rep from * to end.
Repeat 1st to 4th rows until 2 sts remain.
Next row K2tog.
Fasten off.

Join the edgings to the throw

Block each edging following the instructions on page 138 and referring to the ball band.
Attach side edgings to the throw with mattress stitch (see pages 138-9). Join the corners of the side edgings to the corners of the top and bottom edgings with mattress stitch.

FLOWERS

Large roses (Make 24 in various shades of pink Rowan Pure Wool DK)
Using 3.5mm needles cast on 10 sts.
1st row (RS) Knit.
2nd, 4th and 6th rows Purl.
3rd row Knit into front and back of every st. 20 sts.
5th row Knit into front and back of every st. 40 sts.
7th row Knit into front and back of every st. 80 sts.
8th row Purl.
Cast off.
Twist rose into spiral and sew at back to hold in place.

Small roses (Make 60 in various shades of pink Rowan Pure Wool DK and Yarn C)
Using 3.5mm needles cast on 21 sts.
1st to 3rd rows Knit.
Pass all sts one at a time over the first stitch until all stitches are off the RHN except first st.
Fasten off.

Central flowers (Make 12 using Yarn B)
Using 3.5mm needles and Yarn B cast on 5 sts.
1st row Knit into front and back of every st. 10 sts.
2nd and 4th rows Purl.
3rd row Knit into front and back of every st. 20 sts.
5th row Cast off 1 st, * slip st from RHN to LHN needle, cast on 3 sts, cast off 5 sts; rep from * until 1 st remains.
Fasten off.
Using Yarn C embroider 3 or 5 French knots in the centre of the flower (see page 137).

Leaves (Make 60 using Yarn D)
Using 3.5mm needles and Yarn D cast on 5 sts.
1st row (RS) K2, yo, K1, yo, K2. 7 sts.
2nd row and every alternate row Purl.
3rd row K3, yo, K1, yo, K3. 9 sts.
5th row K4, yo, K1, yo, K4. 11 sts.
7th row Ssk, K7, K2tog. 9 sts.
9th row Ssk, K5, K2tog. 7 sts.
11th row Ssk, K3, K2tog. 5 sts.
13th row Ssk, K1, K2tog. 3 sts.
15th row Sl1, K2tog, psso. 1 st.
Fasten off.

FINISHING

Sew a central flower at the centre of each square of the throw.
Sew three small roses in various shades around the central flower and sew three leaves between the small roses.
Sew three large roses of various shades, bunched together, in each corner on the edging of the throw. Sew three leaves between each rose.
Sew three large roses bunched together at the centre of the edging between each corner. Sew three leaves between each rose.
Sew three small roses between each group of large roses around the edging.

feminine fripperies

You can make this gorgeous wrap in either a narrow or wide version, and decorate the lacy edging with ribbon, beads, sequins or buttons. Draped over the end of a bed or the back of a sofa or chair, it will bring a feminine touch to any room. The fine alpaca yarn is very light but hangs beautifully, and feels soft and cosy when wrapped around you.

Scallop-Edged Lace Wrap   Kate Samphier

MATERIALS
8(16) 50g skeins Blue Sky Alpacas Sportweight, shade 528 Vivid Lilac
Pair 5mm (UK 6) knitting needles
Four 70(140)cm/27(55)in lengths of pink silk or taffeta ribbon,
   3cm/1¼in wide
Bugle beads and sequins to decorate

MEASUREMENTS
Width
35.5   70.5cm
14   27½in
Length
170   170cm
67   67in

TENSION
20 sts and 30 rows = 10cm/4in square over garter-stripe pattern
using 5mm needles or the size required to obtain the correct tension.

ABBREVIATIONS
See page 129.

NOTES
The number of stitches changes over the rows.

The wrap/throw is made in two panels, which are grafted together.

WRAP/THROW (Make 2)

Using 5mm needles cast on 93(184) sts.

Work 12 rows in scallop-edge pattern.

1st row (RS) K3, * skpo, sl2, K3tog, p2sso, K2tog, K4; rep from * to last 12 sts, skpo, sl2, K3tog, p2sso, K2tog, K3. 51(100) sts.

2nd row P4, * yo, P1, yo, P6; rep from * to last 5 sts, yo, P1, yo, P4. 65(128) sts.

3rd row K1, yo, * K2, skpo, K1, K2tog, K2, yo; rep from * to last st, K1. 59(115) sts.

4th row P2, * yo, P2, yo, P3, yo, P2, yo, P1; rep from * to last st, P1. 87(171) sts.

5th row K2, yo, K1, * yo, skpo, K1, sl1, K2tog, psso, K1, K2tog, [yo, K1] 3 times; rep from * to last 12 sts, yo, skpo, K1, sl1, K2tog, psso, K1, K2tog, yo, K1, yo, K2. 87(171) sts.

6th row Purl. 87(171) sts.

7th row K5, * yo, sl2, K3tog, p2sso, yo, K7; rep from * to last 10 sts, yo, sl2, K3tog, p2sso, yo, K5. 73(143) sts.

8th to 11th rows Knit. 73(143) sts.

12th row (WS) Purl, inc 0(2) sts evenly across the row. 73(145) sts.

Work 10 rows in eyelet-chevron pattern.

1st row (RS) K4, * K2tog, yo, K1, yo, skpo, K7; rep from * to last 9 sts, K2tog, yo, K1, yo, skpo, K4. 73(145) sts.

2nd, 4th, 6th and 8th rows Purl.

3rd row K3, * K2tog, yo, K3, yo, skpo, K5; rep from * to last 10 sts, K2tog, yo, K3, yo, skpo, K3.

5th row K2, * K2tog, yo, K5, yo, skpo, K3; rep from * to last 11 sts, K2tog, yo, K5, yo, skpo, K2.

7th row K1, * K2tog, yo, K7, yo, skpo, K1; rep from * to end.

9th row K2tog, yo, K9, * yo, sl1, K2tog, psso, yo, K9; rep from * to last 2 sts, yo, skpo.

10th row (WS) Purl.

Next row (RS) Knit, decreasing 4 sts evenly across the row. 69(141) sts.

Work 3 rows in ribbon-eyelet pattern.

1st row (WS) Knit.

2nd row P1, * yo, P2tog; rep from * to end.

3rd row Knit.

Work 13 rows in diamond and eyelet pattern.

1st row (RS) Knit.

2nd, 4th, 6th, 8th, 10th and 12th rows Purl.

3rd row * K4, yo, skpo; rep from * to last 3 sts, K3.

5th row K2, * K2tog, yo, K1, yo, skpo, K1; rep from * to last st, K1.

7th row K1, K2tog, yo, * K3, yo, sl1, K2tog, psso, yo; rep from * to last 6 sts, K3, yo, skpo, K1.

9th row K3, * yo, sl1, K2tog, psso, yo, K3; rep from * to end.
11th row Repeat 3rd row.
13th row (RS) Knit.

Work 3 rows in ribbon-eyelet pattern.
1st row (WS) Knit.
2nd row P1, * yo, P2tog; rep from * to end.
3rd row Knit.
Next row (RS) Knit, increasing 2(0) sts evenly across row. 71(141) sts.
Next row Purl.

Work 28 rows wide leaf border pattern.
1st (RS) and 2nd rows Purl.
3rd row K5, * K2tog, [K1, yo, K1] in next st, ssk, K9; rep from * to end, ending last rep K5 instead of K9.
4th row K5, * P5, K9; rep from * to end, ending last rep K5 instead of K9.
5th row K4, * K2tog, [K1, yo] twice, K1, ssk, K7; rep from * to end, ending last rep K4 instead of K7.
6th row K4, * P7, K7; rep from * to end, ending last rep K4 instead of K7.
7th row K3, * K2tog, K2, yo, K1, yo, K2, ssk, K5; rep from * to end, ending last rep K3 instead of K5.
8th row K3, * P9, K5; rep from * to end, ending last rep K3 instead of K5.
9th row K2, * K2tog, K3, yo, K1, yo, K3, ssk, K3, rep from * to end, ending last rep K2 instead of K3.
10th row K2, * P11, K3; rep from * to end, ending last rep, K2 instead of K3.
11th row K1, * K2tog, K4, yo, K1, yo, K4, ssk, K1; rep from * to end.
12th row K1, * P13, K1; rep from * to end.
13th row K1, * ssk, [K3, yo] twice, K3, K2tog, K1; rep from * to end.
14th row Repeat 12th row.
15th row K1, * yo, ssk, K3, yo, sl1, K2tog, psso, yo, K3, K2tog, yo, K1; rep from * to end.
16th row Repeat 10th row.
17th row K2, * yo, ssk, K7, K2tog, yo, K3; rep from * to end, ending last repeat K2 instead of K3.
18th row Repeat 8th row.
19th row K3, * yo, ssk, K5, K2tog, yo, K5; rep from * to end, ending last repeat, K3 instead of K5.
20th row Repeat 6th row.
21st row K4, * yo, ssk, K3, K2tog, yo, K7; rep from * to end, ending last rep K4 instead of K7.
22nd row Repeat 4th row.
23rd row K5, * yo, ssk, K1, K2tog, yo, K9; rep from * to end, ending last repeat K5 instead of K9.

24th row K6, * P3, K11; rep from * to end, ending last rep K6 instead of K11.
25th row K6, * yo, sl2, K1, p2sso, yo, K11; rep from * to end, ending last rep K6 instead of K11.
26th row Purl.
27th and 28th rows Knit.

Work 4 rows in garter-ridge pattern.
1st row (RS) Knit.
2nd row Purl.
3rd row Knit.
4th row Knit.
Repeat 1st to 4th rows until wrap/throw measures 85cm/33½in from cast-on edge.
Leave these 71(141) sts on a holder.

Work second panel as above, ending on 3rd row instead of 4th row of garter-ridge pattern repeat.

FINISHING
Block each piece following the instructions on page 138 and referring to the ball band.
Kitchener stitch/graft the two panels together and press gently with a warm iron (see pages 139-40).
Randomly stitch beads and sequins between the ribbon-eyelet panels and along the scallop edge on both ends of the wrap/throw.
Thread ribbon through ribbon eyelet panels and secure at each end.

*f*lowers are a favourite motif for feminine interiors and a large pink
bloom brings a sense of delicacy and fragility to this knitted cushion
cover with a matching fluted border. Three layers of petals crafted from
light-as-air Rowan Kidsilk Haze in different shades of deep raspberry and
pale pink are sewn together and decorated with chain-stitch embroidery
and pearl beads, then sewn to the centre of the cushion cover.

Flower Cushion Cover   Nicki Trench

MATERIALS
Three 50g balls Rowan Kid Classic, shade 851 Straw. Yarn A
One 50g ball Rowan Kidsilk Haze, shade 583 Blushes. Yarn B
One 50g ball Rowan Kidsilk Haze, shade 630 Fondant. Yarn C
Small amount of smooth yarn or embroidery yarn for stamens
Pair each 4mm (UK 8) and 5mm (UK 6) knitting needles
Row counter
6 small pearl beads, approximately 4–5mm diameter
5 snap fastenings/press studs
Tapestry needle
Beading needle

MEASUREMENTS
40 x 40cm/16 x 16in square without edging

TENSION
19 sts and 25 rows = 10cm/4in square measured over stocking stitch
using Kid Classic (Yarn A) and 5mm needles or the size required to
obtain the correct tension.

ABBREVIATIONS
See page 129.

CUSHION COVER
Using 5mm needles and Yarn A cast on 76 sts.
1st row (RS) Knit.
2nd row Purl.
Repeating these 2 rows forms stocking stitch.
Repeat 1st and 2nd rows twice.
7th row Knit.
8th row (WS) (first fold line) Knit.
9th to 104th rows Beginning with a knit row work 96 rows st-st.

105th to 108th rows (centre fold line) Knit.
109th to 204th rows Beginning with a knit row work 96 rows st-st.
205th row Knit.
206th row (WS) (third fold line) Knit.
207th to 212th rows Beginning with a knit row work 6 rows in st-st
ending with a purl row.
Cast off.

Cushion side edgings (Make 2)
Using 5mm needles and Yarn A, with RS facing, pick up and knit
202 sts along whole length of side edge.
Cast off all stitches knitways.

FINISHING
Block the cover following the instructions on page 138 and referring
to the ball band.
Fold the cushion cover in half with WS facing each other and the first
and third fold lines meeting at the top. Join side seams with mattress
stitch (see pages 138–9).
Fold the first and third fold lines to the WS so the garter-stitch row
creates the top edge of the cushion and slipstitch the cast-on and
cast-off edges on the inside.
Attach snap fastenings/press studs.

FLOWER (Make 1)
Outer petal
Using 4mm needles and Yarn B cast on 9 sts.
1st row K4, yo, K5. 10 sts.
2nd, 4th, 6th, 8th, 10th, 12th, 14th and 16th rows Knit.
3rd row K4, yo, K6. 11 sts.
5th row K4, yo, K7. 12 sts.
7th row K4, yo, K8. 13 sts.

9th row K4, yo, K9. 14 sts.
11th row K4, yo, K10. 15 sts.
13th row K4, yo, K11. 16 sts.
15th row K4, yo, K12. 17 sts.
17th row K4, yo, K13. 18 sts.
18th row Cast off 9 sts, knit to end. 9 sts.
Repeat 1st to 18th rows 5 times, casting off all sts on the 18th row of the last repeat.
Join cast-off edge to cast-on edge. Weave yarn in and out of centre stitches, pull tight and secure.

Large inner petal

Using 4mm needles and Yarn C cast on 6 sts.
1st row K3, yo, K3. 7 sts.
2nd, 4th, 6th, 8th, 10th, 12th and 14th rows Knit.
3rd row K3, yo, K4. 8 sts.
5th row K3, yo, K5. 9 sts.
7th row K3, yo, K6. 10 sts.
9th row K3, yo, K7. 11 sts.
11th row K3, yo, K8. 12 sts.
13th row K3, yo, K9. 13 sts.
15th row K3, yo, K10. 14 sts.
16th row Cast off 7sts, knit to end. 7 sts.
Repeat 1st to 16th rows 5 times, casting off all sts on the 16th row of the last repeat.
Join cast-off edge to cast-on edge. Weave yarn in and out of centre stitches, pull tight and secure.

Small inner petal

Using 4mm needles and Yarn B cast on 5 sts.
1st row K2, yo, K3. 6 sts.
2nd, 4th, 6th and 8th rows Knit.
3rd row K2, yo, K4. 7 sts.
5th row K2, yo, K5. 8 sts.
7th row K2, yo, K6. 9 sts.
9th row K2, yo, K7. 10 sts.
10th row Cast off 5 sts, knit to end. 5 sts.
Repeat 1st to 10th rows 5 times, casting off all sts on the 10th row of the last repeat.
Join cast-off edge to cast-on edge. Weave yarn in and out of centre stitches, pull tight and secure.

FINISHING

Sew the smaller petals over the larger petals and secure in place as one big flower.
Using a tapestry needle, embroider 6 stamens in chain stitch (5 small chains per stamen), starting from the centre of the flower to halfway up the middle of each small centre inner petal (see page 138). When the 5th small chain on each stamen has been completed, use the beading needle to thread one bead and attach it to the top of the stamen.
Sew the flower onto the centre of the cushion cover.

EDGING

Using 4mm needles and Yarn B cast on 9 sts.
Repeat 1st to 18th rows of the pattern given for the outer petal of the flower 24 times, casting off all sts on the 18th row of the last repeat. Stitch in place around the outside edge of the cushion, 6 points on each of the 4 sides.

Various stitches and yarns have been used to create this luscious circular floor cushion, made up of different-textured segments in mouthwatering shades of orange, pink, lilac and blue. This is a great way to try your hand at new stitches, such as broken rib and blackberry, and it is also a chance to experiment with colour or use up odd balls of yarn from your stash.

Circular Floor Cushion   Nicky Thomson

MATERIALS
Two 100g skeins Manos del Uruguay, shade 2624. Yarn A
Two 50g skeins Blue Sky Alpacas Alpaca Silk, shade 129 Amethyst. Yarn B
Two 100g skeins Manos del Uruguay, shade 2458. Yarn C
Two 50g skeins Blue Sky Alpacas Alpaca Silk, shade 130 Mandarin. Yarn D
Two 100g skeins Manos del Uruguay, shade 2148. Yarn E
Two 100g skeins Noro Kochoran, shade 36. Yarn F
Pair 5mm (UK 6) knitting needles
Small amount of wadding for bobble
Cushion pad, 55cm/22in diameter and 15cm/6in deep
Tapestry needle

MEASUREMENTS
Diameter 51cm/20in
Depth 12.5cm/5in

TENSION
22 sts and 32 rows (16 ridges) = 10cm/4in square measured over garter stitch using two strands of Blue Sky Alpacas Alpaca Silk on 5mm needles or the size required to obtain the correct tension.
22 sts and 24 rows = 10cm/4in square measured over blackberry stitch using Manos del Uruguay on 5mm needles or the size required to obtain the correct tension.
20 sts and 24 rows = 10cm/4in square measured over broken-rib stitch using Manos del Uruguay on 5mm needles or the size required to obtain the correct tension.
24 sts and 24 rows = 10cm/4in square measured over broken-basket stitch using Noro Kochoran on 5mm needles or the size required to obtain the correct tension.

ABBREVIATIONS
See page 129.

COVER TOP (5 triangular sections)

Section 1

Using 5mm needles and two strands of Yarn B cast on 4 sts.

1st row Knit.

2nd and 3rd rows Knit, inc one st at both ends of row. 8 sts.

4th row Knit.

5th row Knit, inc one st at both ends of row. 10 sts.

6th row Knit.

Repeat 5th and 6th rows to 60 stitches.

Cast off 6 stitches at beg of the next 10 rows.

Section 2

Repeat section 1 using Yarn D.

Section 3

Section 3 is worked in blackberry stitch. The basic stitch pattern is as follows:

1st row (RS) Purl.

2nd row * [K1, P1, K1] into next stitch, P3tog; rep from * to end.

3rd row Purl.

4th row * P3tog, [K1, P1, K1] into next stitch; rep from * to end.

The [K1. P1, K1] into next stitch is worked over the previous P3tog, and the P3tog is worked over the previous [K1. P1, K1] into next stitch.

1st to 4th rows form the pattern.

One stitch is increased at both ends of every alternate row while at the same time maintaining the continuity of the blackberry-stitch pattern. The extra '[K1, P1, K1] into next stitch' at the end of every alternate row makes 4 extra stitches.

Using 5mm needles and Yarn A cast on 5 stitches.

1st row and every alternate row (RS) Purl.

2nd row (WS) Inc in first st, [K1, P1, K1] into next st, K1, inc in next st, K1. 9 sts.

4th row Inc in first st, K1, [K1, P1, K1] into next st, P3tog, [K1, P1, K1] into next st, inc in next st, K1. 13 sts.

6th row Inc in first stitch, K1, [[K1, P1, K1] into next st, P3tog] twice, [K1, P1, K1] into next st, inc in next st, K1. 17 sts.

8th row Inc in first stitch, K1, [[K1, P1, K1] into next st, P3tog] 3 times, [K1, P1, K1] into next st, inc in next st, K1. 21 sts.

10th row Inc in first stitch, K1, [[K1, P1, K1] into next st, P3tog] 4 times, [K1, P1, K1] into next st, knit to last 2 sts, inc in next st, K1. 25 sts.

Cont in blackberry stitch, inc one st at each end of every alternate row until 38th row has been worked. 81 sts (18 rows of blackberries).

Cast off 8 sts at beg of next 9 rows. 9 sts.

Cast off remaining stitches.

Section 4

Section 4 is worked in broken-rib stitch. The basic stitch pattern is as follows:

1st row K1, * P1, K1; rep from * to end.
2nd row P1, *K1, P1; rep from * to end.
3rd and 4th rows Knit.
These 4 rows form the pattern.

One stitch is increased at both ends of every alternate row while at the same time maintaining the continuity of the broken-rib-stitch pattern.

Using 5mm needles and Yarn C cast on 3 sts.
1st row (RS) K1, P1, K1.
2nd row Inc in first st, K1, inc in last st. 5 sts.
3rd row Knit.
4th row Inc in first st, knit to last 2 sts, inc in next st, K1. 7 sts.
Cont in broken-rib stitch, inc one st at both ends of every alternate row 15 times while at the same time maintaining the continuity of the pattern. 59 sts.
Cast off 6 sts at beg of next 9 rows. 5 sts.
Cast off remaining stitches.

Section 5

Repeat section 4 using Yarn E.

STRIPED EDGING

Using 5mm needles and Yarn A cast on 22 stitches.
The striped edging is worked in broken-rib stitch.
1st row K1, * P1, K1; rep from * to end.
2nd row P1, * K1, P1; rep from * to end.
3rd and 4th rows Knit.
These 4 rows form the pattern.
Repeat 1st to 4th rows twice. 12 rows worked in Yarn A in all.
Break Yarn A.
Join Yarn C.
Repeat 1st to 4th rows 3 times. 12 rows worked in Yarn C.
Break Yarn C.
Join Yarn E.
Repeat 1st to 4th rows 3 times. 12 rows worked in Yarn E.
Break Yarn E.
Three stripes and 36 rows worked in all.
Repeat these 36 rows 9 times. 30 stripes worked in all.
Cast off using Yarn E.

UNDERSIDE (Make 2)

Using 5mm needles and Yarn F cast on 66 sts.

1st row K2, * P2, K2; rep from * to end.
2nd row P2, * K2, P2; rep from * to end.
Repeat 1st and 2nd rows twice.

Begin basket-stitch pattern.
1st row Knit.
2nd row Purl.
3rd row K2, *P2, K2; rep from * to end.
4th row P2, *K2, P2; rep from * to end.
1st to 4th rows form the pattern.

Work 16 more rows in patt, inc one st at both ends of 4th, 8th, 12th and 16th rows. 74 sts.
Work 8 rows patt without shaping.
Work 38 rows patt, dec one 1 st at both ends of first row and every foll alt row. 36 sts.
Cast off 2 at the beg of the next 4 rows. 28 sts.
Cast off 3 at the beg of the next 4 rows. 16 sts.
Cast off 4 at the beg of the next 2 rows. 8 sts.
Cast off remaining stitches.

BOBBLE

Using 5mm needles and two strands of Yarn B cast on 15 sts.
1st row Knit.
Repeating 1st row forms garter stitch.
Work 19 more rows in g-st.
Cast off and cut yarn leaving a long tail.
Thread the tail through a large tapestry needle and work running stitches all around the outer edge of the square and gather up.
Insert wadding inside and sew up to create a bobble.

FINISHING

Block each piece following the instructions on page 138 and referring to the ball band.
Using Yarn B or Yarn D join the 5 front sections together, creating a circle for the top of the cushion.
Join the cast-on and cast-off ends of the striped edging.
Join the striped edging to the cushion top, 6 edging stripes to each front segment, easing any excess length into the seam.
Overlap the two semicircular pieces for the underside by approx 18cm/7in, with the rib edges towards the centre. The overlap forms the opening for the cushion pad.
Mattress-stitch (see pages 138–9) or backstitch around the curved outer edges to join the pieces together, forming the circle for the underside.
Join the underside of the cover to the other side of the striped edging.
Sew the bobble to the centre of the cover top. Insert the pad.

Lacy-Knit Runner

Emma Seddon

MATERIALS

Three 50g balls Be Sweet Bamboo, shade 627. Yarn A
One 50g ball Be Sweet Bamboo, shade 644. Yarn B
One 50g ball Be Sweet Bamboo, shade 645. Yarn C
One 50g ball Be Sweet Bamboo, shade 613. Yarn D
One 50g ball Be Sweet Bamboo, shade 670. Yarn E
One 50g ball Be Sweet Bamboo, shade 640. Yarn F
One 50g ball Be Sweet Bamboo, shade 651. Yarn G
One 50g ball Be Sweet Bamboo, shade 655. Yarn H
One 50g ball Be Sweet Bamboo, shade 652. Yarn I
Pair each 4mm (UK 8) and 3.75mm (UK 9) knitting needles
Beads and small mother-of-pearl buttons to decorate
Sewing needle and thread

MEASUREMENTS

Width 21cm/8¼in
Length 110cm/43½in
The runner can be made wider by adding extra pattern repeats. For
each pattern repeat cast on an extra 5 stitches. Each pattern repeat
will increase the width by 2.5cm/1in and will need about an extra 12g
of Yarn A. Add more flowers to fill the extra width.

TENSION

20 sts and 30 rows = 10cm/4in square measured over pattern using Yarn
A and 4mm needles or the size required to obtain the correct tension.

ABBREVIATIONS

See page 129.

RUNNER

Using 4mm needles and Yarn A cast on 40 sts.
1st row Purl.
Continue in pattern.
1st row (RS) * K3, yo, K2tog; rep from * to end.
2nd, 4th, 6th and 8th rows Purl.
3rd row Knit.
5th row K3, * K3, yo, K2tog; repeat from * to last 2 sts, K2.
7th row Knit.
These 8 rows form the pattern.
Repeat these 8 rows until runner measures 110cm/43½in, ending
with a WS row.
Cast off.

m ade with silky Be Sweet Bamboo yarn, this beautiful lacy-knit runner, scattered with colourful flowers and leaves, looks gorgeous adorning a shelf, mantelpiece, chest of drawers or dressing table. Make as many or as few of the flowers and leaves as you like. Use up any odds and ends of trimming or buttons or beads that you have, and bring a touch of summer garden into your home.

FINISHING

Block runner following the instructions on page 138 and referring to the ball band.

Work Antwerp stitch (or blanket stitch) around the edges.

LARGE FRONDS/CURLICUES (Make 3 in Yarn F and 2 in Yarn G)

Using 4mm needles cast on 15 sts.

1st row (P1, K1, P1) into each st on the row. 45 sts.

Cast off loosely.

SMALL FRONDS (Make 2 in Yarn F and 2 in Yarn G)

Using 4mm needles cast on 10 sts.

1st row (P1, K1, P1) into each st on the row. 30 sts.

Cast off loosely.

LEAVES (Make 2 in Yarn F and 2 in Yarn G)

Using 4mm needles cast on 3 sts.

1st row and every alternate row to 17th row Purl.

2nd row Knit.

4th row K1, * M1, K1; repeat from * once. 5 sts.

6th row K2, M1, K1, M1, K2. 7 sts.

8th row K3, M1, K1, M1, K3. 9 sts.

10th row K2, K2tog, yo, K1, yo, K2tog tbl, K2. 9 sts.

12th row Repeat 10th row. 9 sts.

14th row K1, sl1, K2tog, psso, yo, K1, yo, K2tog tbl, pass st just worked back to LHN, pick up 2nd st on LHN and pass over first st and drop off LHN, return st knitted back to RHN, K1. 7 sts.

16th row K1, K2tog, K1, K2tog tbl, K1. 5 sts.

18th row K1, sl1, K2tog tbl, psso, K1. 3 sts.

19th row P3tog. 1 st.

Fasten off.

FRILLY EDGE FLOWER - PANSY (Colourway 1 - Make 1)

Using 4mm needles and Yarn D cast on 48 sts.

1st row K1, * K2, slip first st knitted over 2nd st on RHN and drop off; repeat from * to last st, K1. 25 sts.

Break Yarn D.

Join Yarn B.

2nd row P1, * P2 tog; repeat from * to end. 13 sts.

3rd row * K2tog; repeat from * to last st, K1. 7 sts.

Cut yarn, leaving a long tail. Thread the tail through the remaining stitches and pull tightly to create a flower.

Sew in ends and, if necessary, join the seam.

FRILLY EDGE FLOWER - PANSY (Colourway 2 - Make 1)

Using 4mm needles and Yarn E cast on 48 sts.

Break Yarn E.

Join Yarn I.

1st row K1, * K2, slip first st knitted over 2nd st on RHN and drop off; repeat from * to last st, K1. 25 sts.

Break Yarn I.

Join Yarn C.

2nd row P1, * P2 tog; repeat from * to end. 13 sts.

3rd row * K2tog; repeat from * to last st, K1. 7 sts.

Cut yarn, leaving a long tail. Thread the tail through the remaining stitches and pull tightly to create a flower.

Sew in ends and, if necessary, join the seam.

LARGE PICOT KNITTED FLOWER (Make 1 in each of Yarn B, Yarn E and Yarn H)

Using 4mm needles cast on 7 sts.

1st row Cast off 6 sts.

2nd row Cast on 6 sts.

Repeat 1st and 2nd rows 3 times.

9th row Cast off 6 sts. (5 picots made)

Join into a circle by inserting RHN into top of first stitch, wrapping the yarn round the needle and drawing up a stitch (2 sts on RHN). Pass the first stitch over the 2nd stitch, then fasten off the remaining stitch.

SMALL PICOT KNITTED FLOWER (Make 2 in Yarn C, 2 in Yarn D, 2 in Yarn H, 1 in Yarn B and 1 in Yarn E)

Using 4mm needles cast on 5 sts.

1st row Cast off 4 sts.

2nd row Cast on 4 sts.

Repeat 1st and 2nd rows 3 times.

9th row Cast off 4 sts. (5 picots made)

Complete as for picot knitted flower.

KNITTED FLOWER - DAISY (Colourway 1 - Make 1)

Using 4mm needles and Yarn B cast on 57 sts.

1st row Purl.

2nd row K2, * K1, slip this st back onto LHN, pass the next 8 sts on LHN over this stitch and off the LHN, yo2, knit the first st again, K2; repeat from * to end. 27 sts.

3rd row P1, * P2tog, (P1, P1 tbl) into the yo2 of previous row, P1; rep from * to last st, P1. 22 sts.

4th row * K2 tog; repeat from * to end. 11 sts.

5th row Purl.

Thread the tail through the remaining stitches and pull tightly to create a flower. Sew in ends and, if necessary, join the seam.

KNITTED FLOWER - DAISY (Colourway 2 - Make 1)

Using 4mm needles and Yarn C cast on 57 sts.

1st row Purl.

Break Yarn C.

Join Yarn E.

Complete as for knitted flower - Daisy Colourway 1, beginning at 2nd row.

TRUMPET FLOWERS (Make 1 in each of Yarn C, Yarn E and Yarn D)

These flowers begin with a provisional cast-on.

Using 3.75mm needles and a contrasting yarn cast on 14 sts.

1st and 2nd rows Knit.

Break contrasting yarn.

Join main yarn, leaving a long tail.

Work 6 rows st-st beg with a knit row.

9th row K1, * yo, K2tog; repeat from * to last st, K1. 14 sts.

Change to 4mm needles.

Work 5 rows st-st beg with a purl row.

Next row Unravel the contrasting yarn and put the stitches in the main yarn onto a spare 3.75mm needle with the point facing in the same direction as the main needle.

Hold the needles with the stitches parallel, with the WS facing each other. * Using a 3.75mm needle, insert the tip of RHN knitways into the first stitch on the front LHN then knitways into the first stitch on the back LHN and knit both stitches together and off the LHNs.

Rep from * to end of row. 14 sts.

Next row Purl.

Cut yarn, leaving a long tail. Thread tail through the remaining stitches.

Join the side seam with mattress stitch (see pages 138-9).

Pull the stitches together to create a flower and fasten off.

BOBBLE (Make 2 in each of Yarn I and Yarn H)

Using 4mm needles cast on 1 st.

1st row (K1, P1, K1) into same stitch. 3 sts.

2nd row P into front and back of first st, P1, P into front and back of 3rd st. 5 sts.

Work 4 rows st-st beg with a knit row.

7th row K2 tog, K1, K2 tog. 3 sts.

8th row P3tog.

Fasten off.

To create a bobble, use the cast-on and cast-off tails to sew onto the main runner fabric as close together as possible to create a 3-D shape.

BERRY (Make 1 in Yarn B and 1 in Yarn D)

These flowers begin with a provisional cast-on.

Using 4mm needles and a contrasting yarn cast on 14 sts.

1st and 2nd rows Knit.

Break contrasting yarn.

Join main yarn, leaving a long tail.

3rd row Knit. Thread the end left at the beginning of this row through all 14 sts on the needle, leaving the stitches on the needle.

Work 4 rows st-st, beg with a purl row

Break main yarn leaving a long tail. Thread the tail through the stitches on the needle. Remove the contrasting yarn. Pull both tails to gather the stitches then join side seam with mattress stitch. Fasten off.

FINISHING

This pattern has been given as a starting point, but you may prefer to make more of one flower than another, or to substitute beads for the buttons. The colours used, as well as the shape and size of the buttons and/or beads, can vary according to your taste or décor. In addition, each piece, especially the picot knitted flowers and the curlicues, can be varied in length by increasing or decreasing the number of stitches used.

Lay the finished flowers, berries, leaves, beads and buttons on the base fabric, using the photograph as a guide if you wish. When you are happy with their positioning, pin and sew them in place. Threading ribbon through the eyelets horizontally or along each end would create a very feminine touch. Increasing the length of the stitching around the main fabric would allow a narrow ribbon to be threaded through the eyelets created.

the ultimate symbol of love and romance, heart-shaped lavender sachets make lovely presents and can be strewn all around the home. Make as many as you like in lots of different colours and hang them from ribbons on hooks, prop them up on shelves, lay them on the bed or place them inside drawers or cupboards to scent clothes or bed linen. You could even embroider initials or names on the front in chain stitch or running stitch if you wish.

Lavender Heart   Catherine Tough

MATERIALS
One 100g hank Manos del Uruguay, shade 2190 Raspberry. Yarn A
One 100g hank Manos del Uruguay, shade 2148 Rose. Yarn B
Pair 5mm (UK 6) knitting needles
50cm/20in square of bright pink jersey fabric
Sewing machine, needle and matching thread
Dried lavender flowers and funnel
20cm/8in of pink velvet ribbon, 15mm/⅝in wide for the hanging loop

MEASUREMENTS
Width 17cm/6¾in
Length without hanging loop 17cm/6¾in

TENSION
15 sts = 10cm/4in square measured over stocking stitch using 5mm needles or the size required to obtain the correct tension.
11 sts = 10cm/4in square measured over pattern using 5mm needles or the size required to obtain the correct tension.
The correct tension is not a requirement.

ABBREVIATIONS
See page 129.

FRONT
Using 5mm needles and Yarn A make a 23cm/9in square in the following textured stitch.

Cast on 26 sts or the even number of stitches to give the finished width of 23cm/9in.
1st row (WS) Knit.
2nd row (RS) K2, * K1 on row below, K1; rep from * to end.
3rd row Knit.
4th row * K1, K1 on row below; rep from * last 2 sts, K2.
Repeating 1st to 4th rows forms the pattern.
Work in patt until work measures 23cm/9in. Cast off.

BACK
Using 5mm needles and Yarn B make a 23cm/9in square in stocking stitch.
Cast on 35 sts or the number of stitches to give the finished width of 23cm/9in.
Work in stocking stitch until work measures 23cm/9in. Cast off.

FINISHING
Block each piece following the instructions on page 138 and referring to the ball bands, or press with a steam iron and leave to dry. Sandwich the knitting, with right sides facing, between two layers of jersey fabric and pin together; draw a heart shape onto the jersey. Fold the ribbon in half and place the loop in the middle of the heart, with the closed end of the loop pointing downwards between the two layers of knitting. Machine-stitch along the heart outline, leaving a 5cm (2in) gap on one side. Trim away the excess fabric, then turn right side out. Fill the heart with lavender and slipstich the edges of the opening.

No one can resist a pretty iced cake at tea time. Like a giant chocolate cupcake in its jaunty pink-and-white striped case – complete with sugar icing, multicoloured sprinkles and a juicy red cherry on top – this enchanting and whimsical tea cosy will be the focal point of your tea table.

Cupcake Tea Cosy Donna Wilson with Pauline Hornsby

MATERIALS
Two 50g balls Rowan Pure Wool DK, shade 028 Raspberry. Yarn A
One 50g ball Rowan Pure Wool DK, shade 013 Enamel. Yarn B
One 50g ball Debbie Bliss Baby Cashmerino, shade 11 Brown. Yarn C
One 50g ball Rowan Pure Wool DK, shade 041 Scarlet. Yarn D
2-ply embroidery wool in pink, brown, red, green and yellow or
    oddments 100% wool in green and yellow
Pair 3.25mm (UK 10) knitting needles
Pair 4mm (UK 8) knitting needles
Tapestry needle

MEASUREMENTS
Circumference at bottom 46cm/18in
Height (excluding cherry) 22cm/8½in

TENSION
26 stitches and 34 rows = 10cm/4in square measure over stocking
stitch using Baby Cashmerino on 3.25mm needles or the size
required to give the correct tension.
22 stitches and 30 rows = 10cm/4in square measured over stocking
stitch using Pure Wool DK on 4mm needles or the size required to
give the correct tension.
26 stitches and 30 rows = 10cm/4in square measured over striped
pattern using Pure Wool DK on 4mm needles or the size required to
give the correct tension. When stranding the usual yarn at the back
of the work it alters the tension. The act of pulling the yarn behind
will tighten the tension to be the same as for the Baby Cashmerino
yarn (26 sts and 34 rows).

ABBREVIATIONS
See page 129.

NOTES
The tea cosy is made in two identical halves, which are then sewn
together. The pattern starts at the top of the lining and finishes at
the top of the right side of the cosy

When short row shaping, refer to the wrapping technique on page 133.

TEA COSY (Make 2)
Using 4mm needles and Yarn A cast on 33 sts.
1st row (RS of lining) K20, turn.
2nd row P7, turn.
3rd row K11, turn.
4th row P15, turn.
5th row K19, turn.
6th row P23, turn.
7th row K26, turn.
8th row P29, turn.
9th row K31, turn.
10th row Purl all 33 sts.

Beg with a knit row, work 10 rows st-st, inc 1 st at each end of first
row and foll 4 alt rows, ending with a purl row. 43 sts.
Beg with a knit row, work 28 rows st-st, inc 1 st at each end of first,
3rd, 7th and 11th rows, ending with a purl row. 51 sts.

Increase for striped pattern.
Next row (RS) [K3, M1, K4, M1] 7 times, K2. 65 sts.
Lining now completed.

Start striped pattern.
Join Yarn B.
Next row (WS) * P1 Yarn A, P1 Yarn B; rep from * to last st, P1 Yarn A.
Next row (RS) K1 Yarn A, *K1 Yarn B, K1 Yarn A; rep from * to end.
These 2 rows form the striped pattern.
Work 12 more rows in striped pattern.
Break Yarns A and B.

Change to 3.25mm needles.
Join Yarn C.
Beg with a purl row (WS), work 16 rows st-st.
Join Yarn B but do not break Yarn C.
Beg with a purl row and Yarn B, work 2 rows st-st.
Break Yarn B.
Rejoin Yarn C.
Beg with a purl row, work 16 rows st-st, dec 1 st at each end of 6th,
10th, 14th and 16th rows, thus ending with a knit row. 57 sts.
Break Yarn C.

Change to 4mm needles.
Join Yarn B.
1st row (WS) [P2, P2tog] 14 times, P1. 43 sts.
Beg with a knit row, work 10 rows st-st, dec 1 st at each end of first
row and foll 4 alt rows. 33 sts.

Next row (RS) K31, turn.
Next row P29, turn.
Next row K26, turn.
Next row P23, turn.
Next row P23, turn.
Next row K19, turn.
Next row P15, turn.
Next row K11, turn.
Next row P7, turn.
Next row K20, turn.
Cast off all 33 sts loosely purlways.

CHERRY
Using 3.25mm needles and either Yarn A or Yarn B cast on 7 sts.
Work 2 rows in g-st.
Break yarn.

Join Yarn D.
1st row Knit, leaving a long tail. Thread the tail left at the beginning of this
row through all 7 sts on the needle, leaving the stitches on the needle.
2nd row (RS) [K1 then K1 tbl into same stitch] 6 times, K1. 13 sts.
3rd row Purl.
4th row * K1, [K1 then K1 tbl into same stitch]; rep from * 5 times, K1.
19 sts.
5th row Purl.
6th row [K1, K2tog] 6 times, K1. 13 sts.
7th row Purl.
8th row [K2tog] 6 times, K1. 7 sts.
Break Yarn D.
Thread Yarn D through all 7 sts on the needle. Pull firmly to gather
and close, then use the same thread to join the side seam.
Wind Yarn D around first and second fingers of left hand and use
the resulting loop to stuff the cherry.
Remove Yarn A or Yarn B at cast-on. Pull the cast-on tail through
all the stitches on the first row of Yarn D to gather and close,
adjusting stuffing as necessary. Secure thread and leave the tail
for sewing on the cherry.

FINISHING
Block both halves of the cosy following the instructions on page 138
and referring to the ball bands.
PM at side edges between the 14th and 15th rows of the lining,
counting the 20 sts of the first row after the cast-on as the first row.
PM at side edges between the 14th and 15th rows before the cast-off,
counting the 20 sts of the last row before the cast-off as the first row.
PM at side edges between the 9th and 10th rows of the lining,
counting the last row of the lining before the striped pattern as
the first row.
PM at side edges between the 8th and 9th row of the striped
pattern, counting the first row of the striped pattern after the lining
as the first row.

Place both halves of the tea cosy together, wrong sides facing, lining
opposite lining and outer opposite outer.
Join the top (white) section of the outer cosy with mattress stitch
between the markers (see pages 138-9). (Between 14th and 15th rows
on one side edge, the cast-off stitches, and then between 14th and
15th rows on opposite side edge.)
Using 2-ply embroidery wool, embroider straight stitches over the
top white section of the outer to resemble 'hundreds and thousands'.
If preferred, cut lengths of Yarns A, C, D and oddments of green and
yellow yarn and split them into their component threads. Use two
threads of the same colour to embroider.
Join the top section of the lining with mattress stitch between the
markers. (Between 14th and 15th rows on one side edge, the cast-off
stitches, and then between 14th and 15th rows on opposite side edge.)
Join the middle side sections of the cosy with mattress stitch
between the markers, lining to lining and outer to outer.
Sew in as many ends as possible at this stage.
Push the lining into the outer of the cosy.
Join the four seams of the lining to the outer with mattress stitch,
thus leaving holes for the handle and spout.
Attach the cherry to the centre top of the outer, passing the sewing
thread through the centre top of the lining as well as the outer to
keep it in position.

Techniques

Abbreviations

alt	alternate (every other)
cm	centimetre(s)
CN	cable needle
col	colour
beg	begin(ning)
dec	decrease
foll	follow(s)(ing)
g	grams
g-st	garter stitch (knit every row)
in	inch(es)
inc	increase(ing)
inc 1	increase one stitch by working into the front and back of the next stitch
K	knit
K2tog	knit two stitches together
LHN	left-hand needle
M1	make one stitch by picking up the bar between the needles and working into the back of it
mm	millimetres
P	purl
P2tog	purl two stitches together
patt	pattern
PM	place marker
psso	pass slipped stitch over
p2sso	pass two slipped stitches over
rem	remain(ing)
rep	repeat
rev	reverse
RHN	right-hand needle
rnd	round
RS	right side (of work)
skpo	slip one stitch, knit one stitch, pass slipped stitch over
s2kpo	slip two stitches, knit one stitch, pass two slipped stitches over

sl	slip
sl1K	slip one stitch knitways
sl1P	slip one stitch purlways
sl1wyib	slip one stitch with yarn at back of work
sl1wyif	slip one stitch with yarn at/in front of work
sl2wyib	slip two stitches with yarn at back of work
sl2wyif	slip two stitches with yarn at/in front of work
ssk	slip, slip, knit
SM	slip marker
ssp	slip, slip, purl
st-st	stocking stitch (knit on RS rows, purl on WS rows)
st(s)	(stitch)es
tbl	through back of loop(s)
tog	together
WS	wrong side (of work)
yb	yarn back; take yarn to back of work
yf	yarn forward; bring yarn to front of work
yo	yarn over needle or yarn round needle to make a stitch
yo2	yarn over needle or yarn round needle twice to make two stitches
0	No stitches, times or rows

Special abbreviations for individual patterns are included with the pattern.

Charts

Charts give a visual representation of a piece of knitting when completed and also contain the instructions to complete the knitting. Charts can show a complete piece of knitting such as a sleeve, a colour motif or a stitch pattern such as lace or cable.

Charts are made up of squares, where each square represents a stitch. Up the sides of the chart the rows are numbered from 1, at the bottom right, upwards to the last row. Along the bottom of the chart the stitches are numbered from 1, at the bottom right, leftwards to the last stitch.

Charts are read from the bottom row upwards. Right-side rows are read from right to left and wrong-side rows are read from left to right. Wrong-side rows on the chart show how the knitted fabric will look on the right side.

For multicolour knitting, each of the squares contains the colour for that stitch or contains a symbol representing the colour for that stitch. For stitch patterns, such as lace or cable, each of the squares contains a symbol for that stitch. Squares for stitches that are knit on right-side rows and purl on wrong-side rows (stocking stitch) are often left blank. For both multicolour knitting and stitch patterns, a key explains what the symbols mean.

Cast-on

There are many ways to cast on, some using only one needle and some using both, with the stitches cast onto either the right-hand or the left-hand needle. Each method has advantages and disadvantages, and every knitter has their preferred method(s). However, some cast-on methods suit the following stitch pattern, the final uses of the cast-on, such as for picking up stitches, or the wear and tear of the cast-on better than others. Some methods form a decorative edge by themselves.

GERMAN LONG-TAIL CAST-ON (SEE RIGHT)

Also known as the Continental cast-on, this method uses one needle and two strands of yarn. It produces a strong and elastic edge.

1 Place the slip loop on the right-hand needle to make the first stitch. When making the slip loop, leave a tail at least three times the width to be cast on.
2 Hold the ball end and tail yarns in the left hand.
3 Wrap the tail end around the left thumb by moving the thumb clockwise.
4 Lift the ball end with the left forefinger.
5 Insert the tip of the right-hand needle into the strand at the front of the thumb and then insert the needle from top to bottom through the strand on the forefinger.
6 Bring the strand on the forefinger through the strand on the thumb to make a stitch on the right-hand needle.
7 Tighten the strands.
8 Repeat from step 3.

BACKWARD LOOP CAST-ON (SEE FAR RIGHT)

Also known as the Provincial cast-on, twisted loop cast-on or single thumb cast-on, this method uses one needle and a single strand of yarn. It produces a soft edge.

1 Place the slip loop onto the right-hand needle to make the first stitch.

GERMAN LONG-TAIL CAST-ON

2 Close all four fingers of the left hand over the ball end of the yarn, with the end attached to the needle held between the thumb and the left forefinger.
3 Move the thumb from left to right under the needle end of the yarn and wrap the end around the left thumb by moving the thumb clockwise.
4 Insert the tip of the right-hand needle from

BACKWARD LOOP CAST-ON

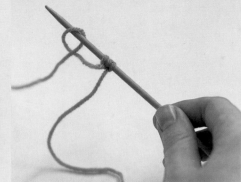

bottom to top into the strand at the front of the thumb and transfer the loop to the needle.
5 Tighten the loop to form the stitch.
6 Repeat from step 3.

CABLE CAST ON (SEE OPPOSITE)

This cast-on method uses two needles and a single strand of yarn. It produces a strong and elastic edge.

1 Place the slip loop on the left-hand needle to make the first stitch.
2 (a) Insert the right-hand needle into the stitch. Wrap the yarn around the tip of the right-hand needle and draw the yarn through to form a loop. OR
(b) Insert the right-hand needle under the left-hand needle to the left of the slip loop. Wrap the yarn around the tip of the right-hand needle and draw it through.
3 Place the loop just made on the left-hand needle to make the next stitch.
4 Insert the right-hand needle between the first two stitches on the left-hand needle. Wrap the yarn around the tip of the right-hand needle and draw the yarn through to form a loop.
5 Place the loop just made on the left-hand needle to make the next stitch.
6 Repeat steps 4 and 5.

CABLE CAST ON

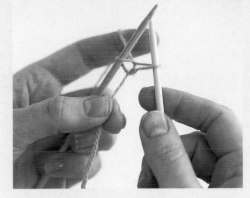

1 Knit the first two stitches.

2 Insert the tip of the left-hand needle into the second stitch on the right-hand needle (the first stitch that was knitted) and lift it over the first stitch on the right-hand needle (the second stitch that was knitted) and off the needle. One stitch has been cast off.

3 Knit the next stitch.

4 Insert the tip of the left-hand needle into the second stitch on the right-hand needle and lift it over the first stitch on the right-hand needle and off the needle.

5 Repeat steps 3 and 4.

6 When casting off all the stitches, when the end of the row is reached, cut the yarn and thread it through the last stitch. Pull the yarn to close the stitch.

7 When casting off at the beginning of a row, after the required number of stitches has been cast off there will be one stitch remaining on the right-hand needle. Complete the remainder of the row as stated in the pattern.

THREE NEEDLE CAST-OFF (SEE RIGHT)

A variation of the standard cast-off, this joins two pieces of knitting together with one cast-off. It produces a neat seam, which is often used at shoulders. When each knitted piece is complete, do not cast off; leave the stitches on a spare needle or a holder.

1 For casting off, the stitches of each piece should be on a needle the same size as that used for the knitting.

2 Place the two pieces right sides together with the stitches at the top and the points of the needles facing in the same direction.

3 Insert the third (empty) right-hand needle knitways into the first stitch of the front piece and then knitways into the first stitch of the back piece and knit them together, slipping both stitches off left-hand needles. One stitch on the right-hand needle.

4 Repeat step 3 for the next stitch from each piece. Two stitches on the right-hand needle.

5 Insert the tip of the left-hand needle into

the second stitch on the right-hand needle and lift it over the first stitch on the right-hand needle and off the needle. One stitch on the right-hand needle.

6 Repeat steps 4 and 5.

7 When all the stitches are cast off, at the end of the row cut the yarn and thread it through the last stitch on the right-hand needle. Pull the yarn to close the stitch.

THREE NEEDLE CAST-OFF

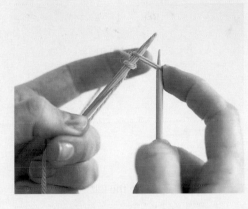

Cast-off

STANDARD OR CHAIN CAST-OFF

Casting off is usually performed knitways (knitting each stitch before casting it off). Sometimes the stitches are cast off purlways or in pattern (working the stitch pattern at the same time as casting off the stitches). The pattern will state the method to use.

Tension

Make the swatch! Make the swatch! Make the swatch! This cannot be emphasized enough. A slight difference in tension for unfitted items such as wraps, throws and toys can fall within acceptable tolerances, but for everything else a tension swatch is essential. Just think of how much time and money you will spend making a beautiful garment, only to find that it is too tight or hangs so loosely it looks dreadful. Making a tension swatch is worth every minute of the half hour or so it takes to knit.

MAKING A TENSION SWATCH

1 Find out from the pattern the number of stitches and rows to 10cm/4in over the stitch pattern.
2 Using the needle size stated in the pattern, cast on the number of stitches to make a swatch 15–20cm/6–8in wide in the stitch pattern.
3 Work the number of rows necessary to make the swatch 15–20cm/6–8in long. Cast off.
4 Block the swatch (see page 138).
5 Pin the swatch to a towel or flat pad, without stretching.
6 Lay a ruler or tape measure across a straight horizontal row of stitches in the middle of the swatch. Place a pin at 0cm/0in and then place a pin at 10cm/4in.
7 Count the number of stitches between the pins.
8 Then lay the ruler or tape measure along a straight vertical line of stitches in the middle of the swatch. Place a pin at 0cm/0in and then place a pin at 10cm/4in.
9 Count the number of rows between the pins.
10 If there are more stitches or rows to 10cm/4in than stated in the pattern, your knitting is too tight. Try again using thicker needles.
11 If there are fewer stitches or rows to 10cm/4in than stated in the pattern, your knitting is too loose. Try again using thinner needles.

Increases

Increases make an extra stitch. They are used when shaping a piece of knitted fabric or for keeping the knitted fabric the same width when starting a stitch pattern that draws in or narrows the knitting, such as cables.

INCREASE 1 OR WORKING INTO THE FRONT AND BACK OF A STITCH

This is a simple method of increasing, but leaves a visible 'bar' at the increase. The 'bar' is formed after the main stitch, so if increasing at both ends of a row, one fewer stitch is worked before the increase at the end of the row than at the beginning of the row in order to keep the number of stitches between the side edge and the 'bar' the same. For example, if three stitches are worked before the stitch with the increase at the beginning of the row, then four stitches will be worked after the increase at the end of the row.

This type of increase is often written as 'inc 1' to distinguish it from other types of increases.

1 Knit or purl the stitch according to the stitch pattern, but do not slip the stitch off the needle.
2 Knit or purl the stitch again through the back of the stitch and slip the stitch just knitted off the left-hand needle.

BAR INCREASE

This is another simple method of increasing. The increases are made between the stitches so that it is easy to keep the number of stitches between the side edge and the increases consistent.

This type of increase is often written as 'M1' to distinguish it from other types of increases.

1 For an increase on the right-hand side of the knitted fabric, insert the left-hand needle from front to back into the bar between the needles and knit or purl into the back of it according to the stitch pattern. The bar will twist when worked to prevent a hole.
2 For an increase on the left-hand side of the knitted fabric, insert the left-hand needle from back to front into the bar between the needles and knit or purl into it according to the stitch pattern. When the left-hand needle is turned to the working position, the bar will twist and, when knitted or purled, will prevent a hole.

Decreases

Decreases remove a stitch. They are used when shaping a piece of knitted fabric or for keeping the knitted fabric the same width when starting a stitch pattern that widens the knitting, such as some lace patterns, or when finishing a stitch pattern that draws in or narrows the knitting, such as cables. When shaping, as for raglans, decreases are worked as paired decreases, where the decreases in each side are mirror images of each other.

KNIT TWO STITCHES TOGETHER

This decrease slopes to the right and is written as 'K2tog'.

1 Insert the right-hand needle knitways into the second stitch on the left-hand needle and then knitways into the first stitch on the left-hand needle.
2 Work a knit stitch through both stitches on the left-hand needle at the same time.

PURL TWO STITCHES TOGETHER

This decrease is used on a purl or wrong-side row where knitting two stitches together would be used on a knit or right-side row. This decrease is written as P2tog.

1 Insert the right-hand needle purlways into the first stitch on the left-hand needle and then purlways into the second stitch on the left-hand needle.
2 Work a purl stitch through both stitches on the left-hand needle at the same time.

SLIP, SLIP, KNIT

This decrease slopes to the left and is written as 'ssk'.

1 Slip the first stitch and the second stitch knitways one at a time from the left-hand needle onto the right-hand needle.
2 Insert the left-hand needle from back to front into these two stitches, with the tip of the left-hand needle in front of the tip of the right-hand needle.
3 Work a knit stitch through both stitches at the same time.

SLIP, SLIP, PURL

This decrease is used on a purl or wrong-side row where slip, slip, knit would be used on a knit or right-side row. This decrease is written as 'ssp'.

1 Slip the first stitch and the second stitch knitways one at a time from the left-hand needle onto the right-hand needle.
2 Return both stitches one at a time to the left-hand needle without twisting them.
3 Insert the right-hand needle purlways into the second stitch on the left-hand needle and then purlways into the first stitch on the left-hand needle.
3 Work a purl stitch through both stitches on the left-hand needle at the same time.

Short rows

'Short rows' is the term for when knitting is turned before the end of the row and the stitches that were then on the right-hand needle only are worked on the next row. This results in more rows being worked on one part of the knitted fabric than on the other. The number of stitches before the turn does not have to be the same every time. Short rows are used for shaping – for example, for shoulders, collars or the heel of a sock.

When the knitting is turned in the middle of the row, a hole appears. This can be avoided by a technique known as 'wrapping' or the 'invisible' turn.

TURNING ON KNIT ROWS

1 Work to the position of the turn.
2 Bring the yarn forward between the needles.
3 Slip the next stitch purlways.
4 Take the yarn back between the needles.
5 Return the slipped stitch to the left-hand needle.
6 Turn the work. The yarn is now in the correct position for purling back, and the slipped stitch is now 'wrapped'.
7 When working the turn on a subsequent row, work the wrap together with the slipped stitch for an 'invisible' turn.

TURNING ON PURL ROWS

1 Work to the position of the turn.
2 Take the yarn back between the needles.
3 Slip the next stitch purlways.
4 Bring the yarn forward between the needles.
5 Return the slipped stitch to the left-hand needle.
6 Turn the work. The yarn is now in the correct position for knitting back, and the slipped stitch is now 'wrapped'.
7 When working the turn on a subsequent row, work the wrap together with the slipped stitch for an 'invisible' turn.

Cables

Cables are much easier to work than they look. Cables are groups of stitches that cross over each other and where the stitches switch places within a row, they make a twist.

Simple cables are worked as columns of stocking stitch, with the cables or twists at regular intervals. Cables are usually worked on a background of reverse stocking stitch, which gives them a raised or three-dimensional effect. The crossing over of the stitches pulls in the knitted fabric, and more stitches are needed than the equivalent width worked in stocking stitch.

The crossing over of the stitches is worked with a cable needle. This is a short knitting needle with points at both ends; it can be straight or cranked (with a wide V shape in the middle). The cable needle should not be thicker than the needles used for the main knitting.

The instructions for cable are written as 'CXB' or 'CXF', where CX refers to the number of stitches to cable and B or F means to cable these stitches to the back or the front. CXB twist to the right and CXF twist to the left.

CABLE STITCHES BACK (SEE BELOW)

1 Slip half the number of stitches stated in CXB onto the cable needle (for example, for C6B slip three stitches onto the cable needle) and hold the cable needle at the back of the work.
2 Knit the remaining half of the number of stitches stated in CXB from the left-hand needle.
3 Knit all the stitches from the cable needle.

CABLE STITCHES (BACK)

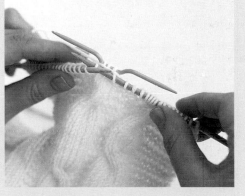

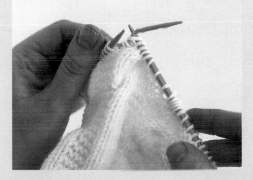

CABLE STITCHES FRONT (SEE BELOW)

1 Slip half the number of stitches stated in CXF onto the cable needle (for example, for C6F slip three stitches onto the cable needle) and hold the cable needle at the front of the work.

2 Knit the remaining half of the number of stitches stated in CXF from the left-hand needle.

3 Knit all the stitches from the cable needle.

Instructions for the cables for the Hot-Water Bottle Cover (pages 90-1) and the Cable Wrap (pages 92-5) are given with those patterns.

CABLE STITCHES (FRONT)

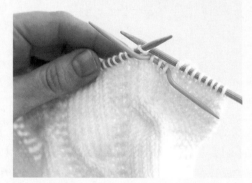

Bobbles (see right)

Bobbles are decorative and can be positioned in many ways – for example, rows, columns, diamonds, lattices or clusters. They can be made in the same or a different colour or yarn from the main knitted fabric and in the same or a different stitch, such as stocking-stitch bobbles on a reverse-stocking-stitch background.

There are many ways of making knitted-in bobbles – some methods making small bobbles and others making large ones. The basic principle is the same: increasing into a single stitch and then decreasing the stitches that have been made to form a bobble on the right side of the knitted fabric, with one or more rows, or perhaps no rows, worked only on the increased stitches before the decreasing.

Bobbles made by decreasing the stitches with no rows between the increased stitches are also known as knots, particularly if only one or a few stitches are increased. Knitting the increased stitches at the same time as the main knitted fabric before decreasing produces a softer bobble.

The increases can be worked by knitting and purling alternately into the same stitch, by knitting into the front and the back of the stitch alternately, or by working a yarn-over between knit stitches. The decreases can be worked by knitting or purling all the stitches together, or slipping some of the stitches, knitting or purling the remaining stitches together and then passing the slipped stitches over.

Bobbles can also be added after knitting. Each bobble is made individually and then sewn on.

Bobbles take up more yarn than the equivalent area of stocking stitch. Pressing bobbles will flatten them, so be careful when blocking.

Patterns always give the instructions for making the type of bobble(s) for that pattern.

BOBBLES

Bead knitting (see below)

Adding beads to knitting adds instant glamour and is easier to do than it looks. Beads can be sewn on after knitting, but this is laborious, and the thread could work loose. Thread all the beads you plan to use onto the yarn before starting to knit. If different types or colours of beads are to be used, make sure they are threaded in the correct order.

BEAD KNITTING

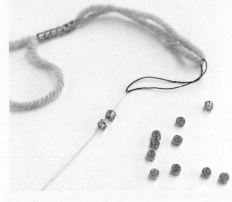

1 Thread a length of sewing thread through the eye of a sewing or beading needle and knot the ends to create a loop; or fold the thread in half to make a loop and thread both cut ends through the needle.
2 Insert the end of the yarn through the loop.
3 Using the needle, thread the beads over the sewing thread and onto the yarn.

POSITIONING A BEAD WITH SLIP STITCH (ON A RIGHT-SIDE ROW)

When knitted in, the beads lie horizontally.

1 Hold the yarn at the front of the work, bringing the yarn forward between the needles if necessary.
2 Push the bead as close as possible to the right-hand needle.
3 Slip the next stitch purlways so that the bead is positioned in front of this stitch.
4 Continue the row, taking the yarn back between the needles if necessary.

Buttonholes

There are several ways to make a buttonhole, the chosen method being determined partly by the size of the button and by the amount of wear and tear the buttonhole will have. Buttonholes should be large enough to allow the button to pass through, but not so large that the button keeps coming undone.

Patterns give instructions for the position of buttonholes and usually how to make the buttonholes for that pattern.

HORIZONTAL BUTTONHOLE

The horizontal buttonhole is worked over two rows. On the first row, stitches are cast off at the position of the buttonhole, and on the second row the same number of stitches are cast on over the cast-off stitches.

VERTICAL BUTTONHOLE

The vertical buttonhole is worked in two parts. The first row is worked to the position of the buttonhole. Instead of working to the end of the row, the work is turned at this point and these stitches only are worked for the length of the buttonhole. The stitches on the other side of the buttonhole are then worked for the same number of rows. On the next row all the stitches are worked and knitting continues over all stitches to the next buttonhole.

EYELET BUTTONHOLE (SEE BELOW)

The eyelet buttonhole is suitable for small buttons and is used mainly on babies' and children's garments. It is worked over one row as 'yarn over, work two stitches together' or 'work two stitches together, yarn over'. Working two stitches together (a decrease) next to the yarn-over (an increase) keeps the stitch count correct. A larger eyelet buttonhole can be made by wrapping the yarn twice around the needle instead of once at the yarn-over and dropping the extra loop – to make a larger hole – on the next row.

EYELET BUTTONHOLE

Eyelets (see below)

Eyelets are individual holes in knitted fabric, which can be worked as a row or worked into a pattern over several rows, usually on the right side of a stocking-stitch, reverse-stocking-stitch or garter-stitch background. They are characterized by their 'yarn over, work two stitches together' type stitch pattern. As for the eyelet buttonhole, the yarn-over increase is compensated for by the work-two-stitches-together decreases to maintain the stitch count.

A line of eyelets – horizontal, vertical or diagonal – makes holes in which to insert a ribbon, cord or elastic (but never around the necks of babies' or children's garments). The eyelets can be spaced close together, far apart or in a close-far pattern. The background may be rib or another stitch pattern, but preferably not one that is likely to become muddled with the eyelets.

Working eyelets as 'yarn over, knit two stitches together' – the increase first – gives a bias to the right. Working eyelets as 'knit two stitches together, yarn over' – the increase last – gives a bias to the left. 'Slip, slip, knit' or equivalent decreases can be worked instead of 'knit two stitches together'.

EYELETS

Ways to embellish

I-CORD (KNITTED CORD)

I-cords are circular cords knitted on two double-pointed needles. The result is similar to the cords obtained with French knitting or bobbin knitting. Advantages of knitting I-cords on two needles include using any yarn on any size needles to suit your project, choosing the thickness of the I-cord by having from two to seven stitches (depending on yarn and/or needle thickness) and accurate measurement of length.

Among other uses, I-cords can be used as ties as an alternative to ribbon, or for sewing onto knitted or other fabric to make frog fastenings or raised designs, or for hanging pompoms, tassels or mobiles.

MAKING AN I-CORD (SEE RIGHT)

1 Using two double-pointed needles cast on from two to seven stitches.
2 Knit these stitches from the left-hand needle to the right-hand needle.
3 Without turning the needle, push the stitches to the other end of the right-hand needle.
4 Without turning the needle, transfer the needle to the left hand and hold the needle ready to knit the stitches again. The yarn will be hanging at the left of the stitches.
5 Bring the yarn behind the stitches and knit the stitches from the left-hand needle to the right-hand needle.
6 Repeat steps 3 to 5.
7 To finish, either cast off or break the yarn, thread the yarn through the stitches and pull to gather.
8 Sew in the ends.

Commercial French-knitting bobbins and dollies are widely available, usually with four prongs, but some are available with a greater number of prongs. If using a commercial bobbin or dolly, follow the instructions provided.

MAKING AN I-CORD

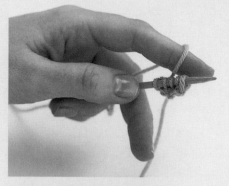

FRINGES

Fringes are often used at the end of scarves and around the edges of shawls. The tassels should be attractively spaced and even in length. You can make the fringe as thin or thick as you like by varying the number of strands.

MAKING A SIMPLE FRINGE (SEE OPPOSITE)

1 Cut the yarn into pieces about two-and-a-half times the length of each tassel. Do this by wrapping the yarn around a suitable-sized book and then cutting at one or both ends.
2 With the right side of the knitted fabric facing, insert a crochet hook from back to front at the position of the tassel.
3 Take a group of strands half the thickness of the tassel. Fold the stands in half and wrap the folded end around the crochet hook.
4 Pull the hook from front to back, taking the folded end of the group of strands with it through the knitted fabric to make a loop.

MAKING A FRINGE

5 Thread the cut ends of the strands through the loop and pull gently to secure the knot.
6 When all the tassels have been made, make sure they are even and then trim the ends to the same length.

POMPOMS

Pompoms make simple decorative features to use on the top of hats, on the back of gloves, at the end of cords, or just sewn on wherever.

Commercial pompom-making kits are available with templates in three or four sizes. If using one of these kits, follow the instructions provided.

MAKING A POMPOM (SEE RIGHT)

1 On a piece of stiff card or plastic, draw a circle with the diameter of the pompom you wish to make. Either use a compass or draw around a circular object, such as a cup.

MAKING A POMPOM

2 In the centre of the circle, draw a smaller circle with a diameter one-third to one-half the diameter of the larger circle. The thicker the yarn, the larger the inner circle needs to be.
3 Cut around the outline of the larger circle, then cut out the inner circle.
4 Make another piece in the same way, and place the two circles together.
5 Thread a tapestry needle with your chosen

yarn. Take the needle around and around the ring, adding new lengths of yarn as required.
6 When the ring is completely covered with yarn and the hole filled, use sharp scissors to cut the yarn at the outer edge of the circles.
7 Gently pull the two circles away from each other so as not to disturb the cut strands.
8 Wind another length of yarn between the circles, around the centre core of the strands, and knot firmly. If sewing on the pompom, leave the ends of this thread uncut.
9 Remove the two card or plastic circles.
10 Fluff out the pompom and trim stray ends.

EMBROIDERY

Embroidery is best worked after blocking and with a yarn that is not so thick as to distort the knitted fabric. Do not work the embroidery stitches too tightly, and block the knitted fabric again after embroidering.

FRENCH KNOTS (SEE BELOW)

1 With the right side of the knitted fabric facing, bring the sewing needle, threaded with the yarn for the knot, through from back to front at the position of the knot.
2 Hold the needle close to where it emerged and wind the yarn once or twice around the tip.
3 Keeping the loop(s) in place, take the needle from front to back immediately next to where the needle first came through; pull the thread through the loop(s) quickly and smoothly, and fasten on the wrong side.

FRENCH KNOTS

CHAIN STITCH

CHAIN STITCH (SEE ABOVE)

When worked in a circle with the bottom of the stitches all starting in the centre, this stitch suggests the petals of a flower and is called lazy daisy stitch.

1 With the right side of the fabric facing, bring the threaded tapestry needle through from back to front at the position of the bottom of the first stitch.
2 Form the yarn into a loop; insert the needle from front to back where it first emerged.
3 Bring the needle up through the fabric again, from back to front, inside the loop at the top of the stitch.
4 Pull the yarn through, but not too tightly, so that the loop is gently rounded and the knitted fabric remains flexible.
5 Take the needle down again inside the loop, where it emerged in step 3, forming a new loop.
6 Repeat steps 3–5.

Weaving in ends

There is no one correct way to weave in ends, but they should be woven in neatly and not seen on the right side of the knitted fabric, leave no holes, have no knots and, in multicolour knitting, be woven into their own colour. When possible, join new balls of yarn at the beginning of a row, but not if that edge is a free edge (not taken into a seam). The ends can be sewn into the edge of the knitted stitches inside the seam, sewing one end upwards and one end downwards.

Leave a long end for weaving in and make sure the end is secure before cutting it, especially with yarns that easily fray or unravel.

When joining yarn in the middle of a row, such as for multicolour knitting, the ends should be sewn in before blocking. Using a sharp sewing needle will split the stitches in the wrong side and help make the weaving in less visible on the right side. Close holes or complete stitches by sewing the end through the adjacent stitch to complete the stitch as if it had been knitted. Ends can also be woven in by following the interlocking lattice of the knitted stitches on the wrong side.

Blocking

Blocking is pinning out a piece of knitted fabric to the correct size and shape, then pressing or damp finishing before sewing up. Blocking gives a smooth finish and proper shape to the knitted fabric, stretching edges that are pulling, sharpening points and corners, and drawing buttonhole slits together. Knitted pieces should be blocked before sewing up, and all mid-row ends should be woven in.

Blocking is done on a blocking pad laid on a firm, flat surface, such as an ironing board, kitchen table or floor. The blocking pad should be well padded – an old blanket covered with a white cloth or a large folded clean towel will suffice. Pins should be rustless and with glass or other highly visible heads. Err on the side of generosity when using pins.

Read the ball band for the yarn to check the pressing instructions. If using more than one yarn, follow the gentlest method of pressing or use the damp-finishing method. Do not press rib, raised patterns or stitch patterns that would be flattened. Damp finishing is recommended for the novice or the nervous.

PINNING OUT

With the wrong side of the knitting uppermost, pin out each piece along the edges to size and shape, making sure that the rows and the columns of stitches are straight. The pins should be at right angles to the knitting, from the outer edge inwards. Do not pin out ribs (unless told to do so) and let the knitting narrow naturally towards ribbed areas.

PRESSING

1 Cover the knitted piece with a white cloth. As a general rule, use a dry cloth for synthetics and a damp cloth for natural fibres, both with a dry iron. Be guided by the pressing instructions on the ball band.
2 Heat the iron to the correct temperature, as stated on the ball band.
3 Put the iron on the cloth and immediately lift it up again. Repeat all over the knitted piece. Never use an ironing motion.
4 Leave the cloth in place until cool and/or dry.

DAMP FINISHING

1 Fill a spray bottle with cold water and lightly spray the knitted piece until damp, avoiding ribs.
2 Cover with a clean white cloth and pat gently to absorb excess water.
3 Remove the cloth and allow the knitted piece to dry naturally.

Sewing up

MATTRESS STITCH (SEE OPPOSITE)

Joining knitted pieces using mattress stitch, also known as ladder stitch or the invisible seam, gives a neat seam and can be used to join most knitting stitches, including stocking stitch, reverse stocking stitch and rib. Sewing is done on the right side of the knitted fabric, making it easier to match shapings, pattern repeats and stripes. A full stitch is usually taken into the seam, but half a stitch can be taken in for thick yarns. When joining seams with the same number of rows or stitches on each side, it is not necessary to pin the pieces together.

1 Place the pieces to be joined side by side with the right side uppermost.
2 Start at the bottom (cast-on) edge. Bring the threaded sewing needle from the cast-on corner of the right-hand piece, insert from back to front between the first and second cast-on stitches of the left-hand piece, then from back to front between the first and second cast-on stitches of the right-hand piece and then back again from back to front between the first and second cast-on stitches of the left-hand piece. This makes a figure-of-eight and neatly closes the start of the seam.
3 Between each stitch is a 'bar' made by the yarn. Pick up the bar between the first and second stitch on the first row of the right-hand piece.
4 Pick up the bar between the first and second stitch on the first row of the left-hand piece.
5 On the right-hand piece, insert the needle where it came out and pick up the next bar.

MATTRESS STITCH

6 On the left-hand piece, insert the needle where it came out and pick up the next bar.
7 Repeat steps 5 and 6. Every 2–3 cm, pull the sewing yarn firmly to close the seam.

Cast-off and cast-on edges can be joined by taking in one stitch or a half stitch into the seam instead of the 'bar'. If the yarn is not pulled too tightly, the seaming forms a row of knit stitches.

GRAFTING STOCKING STITCH

Mattress stitch can also be used for joining a cast-on or cast-off edge to a side edge, or when gathering a longer edge to fit a shorter one. Pinning the pieces together will help to keep them evenly matched. Where necessary, pick up two or more bars or stitches instead of one.

KITCHENER STITCH/GRAFTING

This joins two sets of stitches that haven't been cast off, so that the join looks like continuous knitting. Stitches from a provisional cast-on can also be grafted. Stitches not cast off or provisional cast-on stitches can also be grafted to a cast-off edge, a cast-on edge or a side edge. For the following methods, both needles have the tips pointing to the right.

GRAFTING STOCKING STITCH (SEE LEFT)

1 Lay the knitted pieces knit side up on a flat surface, needle to needle, needles horizontal. Remove some or all stitches from the needles.
2 Thread a tapestry needle with an end-of-row tail from one of the knitted pieces or a new length of yarn (contrast yarn shown here).
3 Working from right to left, insert the tapestry needle from back to front through the first stitch from the bottom needle.
4 Insert the tapestry needle from front to back through the first stitch from the top needle.
5 Insert the tapestry needle from back to front through the next stitch from the top needle.
6 Insert the tapestry needle from front to back through the first stitch from the bottom needle.
7 Insert the tapestry needle from back to front through the next stitch from the bottom needle. One stitch completed. Adjust the tension of the stitch to match the knitting.
8 Repeat steps 4 to 7.

GRAFTING FROM TWO NEEDLES

1 Hold the needles together with the purl sides of the knitted pieces facing each other.
2 Thread a tapestry needle with an end-of-row tail from one of the knitted pieces or a new length of yarn.
3 Working from right to left, insert the

tapestry needle from back to front through the first stitch on the front needle. Pull the yarn through and leave the stitch on the needle.

4 Insert the tapestry needle from front to back through the first stitch on the back needle. Pull the yarn through and leave the stitch on the needle.

5 Insert the tapestry needle from front to back through the first stitch on the front needle and slip the stitch off the needle.

6 Insert the tapestry needle from back to front into the next stitch on the front needle and leave the stitch on the needle.

7 Insert the tapestry needle from back to front into the first stitch on the back needle and slip the stitch off the needle.

8 Insert the tapestry needle from front to back into the next stitch on the back needle and leave the stitch on the needle.

9 Repeat steps 5 to 8.

SWISS DARNING/COVER STITCH

This mimics stocking stitch and is often used to work a small area of colour, such as letters, numbers or a motif. The tapestry needle is inserted in the spaces between the stitches, not into the yarn. The embroidery yarn should be compatible with the knitted fabric and of a thickness to cover the knitted stitch.

1 Hold the fabric with the knit side uppermost; thread a tapestry needle with embroidery yarn.

2 Insert the needle from back to front through the centre of the stitch below the stitch to be covered. This is the centre bottom of the stitch to be covered.

3 Following the path of the stitch, insert the needle from front to back at the top right or top left of the stitch – top right if you are working from right to left and vice versa.

4 Take the needle behind the stitch and then bring it through from back to front.

5 Insert the needle from front to back into the place where it started. The needle and yarn have traced the path of the stitch to be covered.

6 Repeat steps 2 to 5.

Suppliers

Loop
41 Cross Street, Islington,
London N1 2BB, UK
Tel: +44 (0)20 7288 1160
www.loop.gb.com
All of the yarns and haberdashery shown in this book are available at Loop and Loop's online shop. We ship worldwide.

Contact the following suppliers or check their websites for stockist information.

YARN

Alchemy Yarns
PO Box 1080, Sebastopol, CA 95473, USA
Tel: +1 707 823 3276
www.alchemyyarns.com

Be Sweet
1315 Bridgeway, Sausalito, CA 94965, USA
Tel: +1 415 331 9676
www.besweetproducts.com

Blue Sky Alpacas
PO Box 88, Cedar, MN 55011, USA
Tel: +1 888 460 8862
www.blueskyalpacas.com

Colinette
Banwy Workshops, Llanfair Caereinion,
Powys, Wales SW21 0SG, UK
Tel: +44 (0)1938 810 128
www.colinette.com

Designer Yarns
Unit 8-10 Newbridge Industrial Estate, Pitt Street,
Keighley, West Yorkshire BD21 4PQ, UK
Tel: +44 (0)1535 664 222
www.designeryarns.uk.com
Debbie Bliss, Louisa Harding and Noro.

Frog Tree
T&C Imports, PO Box 1119, 14 Frog Tree Lane,
East Dennis, MA 02641, USA

Tel: +1 508 385 8862
www.frogtreeyarns.com

ggh
Mühlenstraße 74, 25421 Pinneberg, Germany
Tel: +49 (0)4101 208 484
www.ggh-garn.de

Habu Textiles
135 West 29th Street, Suite 804, New York,
NY 10001, USA
Tel: +1 212 239 3546
www.habutextiles.com

Jade Sapphire
148 Germonds Road, West Nyack,
NY 10994, USA
Tel: +1 866 857 3897
www.jadesapphire.com

KnitGlobal
AC Wood Specialty Fibres, CCL House,
Inmoor Road, off Cross Lane, Tong,
Bradford BD11 2PS, UK
www.knitglobal.com

Knit One Crochet Too
91 Tandberg Trail, Unit 6, Wyndham,
ME 04062, USA
Tel: +1 800 357 7646
www.knitonecrochettoo.com

Lana Grossa
Heritage Stitchcraft Ltd, Redbrook Lane,
Brereton, Rugeley, Staffs WS15 1QU
Tel: +44 (0)1889 575 256
www.lanagrossa.com

Lantern Moon
7911 NE 33rd Drive, Suite 140, Portland,
OR 97211, USA
Tel: +1 800 530 4170
www.lanternmoon.com
Leigh Radford's Silk Gelato yarn.

Manos Del Uruguay

Sarl Distrilaine, 5 rue Thomas Edison,

44470 Carquefou, France

Tel: +33 (0)8 73 65 44 06

www.distrilaine.com

Ozark Handspun

PO Box 1405, Jefferson City,

MO 65102-1405, USA

Tel: +1 573 644 8736

www.ozarkhandspun.com

PluckyFluff

Web: www.pluckyfluff.com

Unique handspun yarns.

Rowan

Green Lane Mill, Holmfirth HD9 2DX, UK

Tel: +44 (0)1484 681 881

www.knitrowan.com

Rowan, Jaeger and Gedifra yarns.

CUSHIONS

Allshapes Cushions Ltd

Unit 29, Vernon Building, Westbourne Street,

High Wycombe, Bucks HP11 2PX, UK

Tel: +44 (0)1494 465 581

www.allshapes.co.uk

This company will make pads to any size and are very reliable; they also have a helpful website.

LAVENDER

Norris & Armitage

3 Brooklands Road, Bedhampton, Havant,

Hants PO9 3NS, UK

Tel: +44 (0)2392 718 914

www.lavendersupplies.co.uk

Two varieties of totally natural chemical-free dried lavender from Provence, sold in resealable bags from 250g to 10kg.

BEADS

Check the Internet, as there are a lot of online shops that sell all kinds of beads.

Creative Beadcraft

20 Beak Street, London W1F 9RE, UK

Tel: +44 (0)20 7629 9964

www.creativebeadcraft.co.uk

Beads, sequins and trims.

BUTTONS

Besides being functional, buttons can be used as embellishments. You can use one stunning huge one with other smaller elements (such as small buttons, tiny pompoms or beads), or use beautiful vintage buttons in clusters or scattered along an edge. For unusual or vintage examples, try vintage-textile fairs, which are usually advertised in local papers or craft and textile magazines such as Crafts and Selvedge. In London, Portobello Market is good for finds, as well as the Vintage Textile Fair at Hammersmith Town Hall a few times a year. You can also mooch around flea markets, jumble sales and secondhand shops. Sometimes it's worth looking at secondhand clothing just to see if the buttons are interesting – you can cut them off and use them for your new piece. Ebay is also a very good source for vintage buttons and trims.

The Button Queen

19 Marylebone Lane, London W1V 2NF, UK

Tel: +44 (0)20 7935 1505

www.thebuttonqueen.co.uk

Tender Buttons

143 E 62nd Street, New York, NY 10021, USA

Tel: +1 212 758 7004

They don't have an online shop (pity for us), but there is no way I could leave out this complete gem of a shop. It is, quite simply, the best button shop I have ever been to in the world. If you are ever anywhere near NYC, make a beeline for it.

RIBBONS AND TRIMS

Temptation Alley

359/361 Portobello Road, London W10 5SA, UK

Tel: +44 (0)20 8964 2004

www.temptationalley.com

Very helpful and friendly shop offering an amazing selection of very reasonably priced ribbons, trims, tassels, beads, feathers, sequins and lace. They ship worldwide.

V V Rouleaux

102 Marylebone Lane, London W1U 2QD, UK

Tel: +44 (0)20 7224 5179

www.vvrouleaux.com

Fantastic selection of ribbons and trims. There are also V V Rouleaux shops in Sloane Square, Glasgow and Newcastle.

PURSE CLASPS AND BAG HANDLES AND FRAMES

Lacis

3163 Adeline Street, Berkeley, CA 94703, USA

Tel: +1 510 843 7178

www.lacis.com

Fabulous selection of the most exquisite bag and purse frames and handles. They have vintage Lucite and other beauties.

U-Handbag

150 McLeod Road, London SE2 0BS, UK

Tel: +44 (0)208 310 3612

www.U-handbag.com

A useful website selling bag and purse frames, as well as bamboo, wood, metal and plastic bag handles of all shapes and sizes.

Designers' Biographies

Julie Arkell is one of Britain's foremost contemporary folk artists. An avid collector, she recycles 'the rejected debris of everyday life', using paper from old books, fabrics from vintage clothes, and objects that have been sourced from her local hardware and haberdashery stores. Julie employs traditional techniques, such as papier-mâché, stitching, knitting, painting, embroidery and collage, and through these evolving processes her exquisite 'creatures' are made.

Debbie Bliss studied fashion and textiles at art college before becoming a knitwear designer. She has published more than 25 books of hand-knit designs for adults and children, and in 1999 she launched her own range of yarns.

When designing, Debbie loves to play with texture, combining, for example, the diagonals of a cable with the simplicity of a moss-stitch panel and using decorative stitch details to enhance a basic design. When she launched her own yarn range, it was natural to lean towards the classic smooth yarns, which clarify texture and stitch, and to use beautiful fibres such as cashmere, alpaca, silk and fine merino.
www.debbieblissonline.com

Ruth Cross was founded in 2004 by Ruth Bridgeman after she graduated with a degree in Fashion Textile Design from the University of Brighton. Her focus now is to rethink the traditional capabilities of handknitting to create beautiful contemporary pieces. Unconcerned by homogeneous trends, Ruth's creations are highly desirable; the stitches and techniques used are often unique to Ruth Cross, which makes their patterns highly distinctive and unusual. These pieces are impossible to copy using machines – for Ruth, it is all about the individual and their creative part in the process.
www.ruthcross.com

Nadine Curtis founded Be Sweet in 2003 while living in Cape Town, South Africa. Her previous experience in design and passion for socially conscious programmes served as catalysts for turning her fascination with handmade accessories into a thriving business, which supports local women artisans in South Africa.

Be Sweet makes six different styles of luxury mohair in various blends, including brushed, bouclé and baby mohair yarn. All yarn is hand-dyed and handspun, and many are offered in more than 60 solid colours and 15 handpainted colours. Select balls are accented with delicate ribbons, metallic strands and African beads.

Bardet Wardell graduated from Rhode Island School of Design Apparel and held design positions in New York City with dress and sportswear manufacturers before producing her own labels, Bardet and Everyday Goddesses. With the advent of Be Sweet, Bardet has focused on creating patterns that are both beautiful and simple to execute with the unique yarns produced in South Africa.
www.besweetproducts.com

Kristeen Griffin-Grimes is a designer based in Washington State and creator of French Girl's hallmark style of knit and crochet patterns: ethereal, draped garments superbly fitting to the feminine form. French Girl patterns are constructed in a unique manner, the garments fashioned in one piece from start to finish. Using her seamstress and costuming background, Kristeen begins her design process almost architecturally, to deconstruct her envisioned garment and reconstruct it again in a more organic way, either from the top down, from the hem up, or from the back out.

The designer's aesthetic is rooted in her early years as a 'nature girl' on her family's oyster farm on the rural Pacific Northwest coast.
www.frenchgirlknits.com

Louisa Harding studied Textiles for Fashion at Brighton University. During her third year she undertook a placement at Rowan Yarns, who published two of her very early designs. After working in Canada she returned to England, where she worked as in-house designer for Rowan Yarns, selecting yarns, writing patterns, and contributing to its publications.

Since having children, she has been working alongside her husband Stephen, a photographer. Together they created the Miss Bea series of knitting books. As a result of the Miss Bea series, Louisa was given the opportunity of introducing her own line of yarns and pattern publications in 2005. She thoroughly enjoys the creative experience of playing with colour and texture, and designing beautiful knitwear patterns.
www.louisaharding.co.uk

Claire Montgomerie has an MA in Constructed Textiles from the Royal College of Art, London. She has a wealth of experience in the craft and textile industries and runs a successful online business selling her quirky knitted wares. Claire teaches knitting classes at Loop, children's textile courses at the artsdepot, London, and textile jewellery courses at West Dean College, Sussex.

Claire is the author of *Easy Baby Knits* and the co-author of *London Crochet*. She has also contributed designs to *Hookorama*, *Instant Expert Crochet* and *Loop: Vintage Crochet*.
www.clairemontgomerie.com

Leigh Radford is an award-winning author, designer and teacher living in the Pacific Northwest. Her books include the highly popular *AlterKnits: Imaginative Projects and Creativity Exercises* and *One Skein: 30 Quick Projects to Knit & Crochet*.

In 2006 Leigh created Silk Gelato, offering knitters a fibre with enhanced texture and plays of colour for her unique pattern designs. Her enterprising efforts have resulted in a highly successful business collaboration with Lantern Moon, producers of Silk Gelato.

Leigh is in demand for her innovative classes and workshops. She enjoys teaching others the value of being creative and is inspired by the expression of original ideas that lend a fresh perspective to knitting and crochet.
www.leighradford.com

Kate Samphier was inspired by traditional knitting in Scotland, and her collections embrace Scottish knitwear manufacture, challenging tradition with an eclectic use of colour, texture and pattern.

After studying textiles in the Scottish Borders, Kate worked for a local woollen spinner for five years as a yarn and knit-fabric designer. Drawn to the raw material and colours that she worked with, Kate began to create her own knitted accessories to illustrate the versatility of the company's yarn ranges.

In Spring 2000 Kate set up her design studio and workshop. The following year, her first collection of knitted accessories was launched. Featured in magazines such as *Easy Living*, *Homes and Gardens*, *Junior* and *Selvedge*, Kate's designs are for women with an eye for beauty and a quirky sense of style.
www.katesamphier.co.uk

Leslie Scanlon lives in a small New England coastal town with her husband and two children. She has been designing knitwear for ten years under the MAC & MF label. Her pieces are designed with clear colours and minimalist shapes in mind. Leslie combines elegant details with contemporary design to make timeless pieces.
www.macandme.net

Emma Seddon was taught to knit by her grandma, and has never looked back. She trained at Central St Martins School of Art, where she did a Knitted Textiles degree. Working for the next 12 years on a variety of different textiles products, she spent most of her free time knitting, crocheting and sewing, taking the odd spare moment to peruse charity shops for patterns and balls of yarn.

In 2004 she became freelance, to pursue her first loves of knitting and crochet, and to inspire others to do the same, through teaching. She works with Rowan as a freelance design consultant, teaches at local colleges and works on a wide range of design projects.

Nicky Thomson was inspired to knit as a young girl by her grandmother, Nellie Callear, having been enthralled by the clickety-clicks of her knitting needles and seeing the fabric magically appear. She loved rummaging in her grandmother's box of threads, buttons and yarns, and learnt to use her old Singer sewing machine and knit her first jumper. Totally hooked on textiles and yarns, Nicky later studied for a BA in Textiles Design, specializing in woven and knitted fabrics. On graduating, she worked as an interior designer, but spent her free time designing and knitting.

In creating her designs, she constantly investigated colour, pattern, the surface qualities of threads and finishing techniques. She now works with a small UK manufacturing company to produce ever-changing collections, which are individually made and finished, and are sold worldwide.
www.nickythomson.com

Catherine Tough established her interior accessory design company in 2000 after graduating from the Royal College of Art, London. She sells her work throughout the UK and internationally. Much of the appeal of Catherine's knitwear comes from her reworking of traditional items and knitting patterns in luxury yarns, and revitalizing them with her contemporary stylings.

Catherine lives in Hackney, London, where she draws inspiration from the vibrant mix of urban cultures. Since her daughter Abigail was born, she has rediscovered much of her sense of colour and playfulness, which first came from children's books, illustration and imagination, and from her own rural Worcestershire childhood. This gives an intimate and friendly feel to her products, which appeal to adults and children alike. She has published two books, *Hip Knits* and *Easy Knits for Little Kids*.
www.catherinetough.co.uk

Nicki Trench founded Laughing Hens, a UK mail-order knitting website, which has captured a new wave of interest in knitting as a modern creative hobby for women. Nicki has written two books, *The Cool Girl's Guide to Knitting* and *The Cool Girl's Guide to Crochet*, and is currently writing a third, *The Cool Girl's Guide to Sewing*.

Nicki's inspiration has always been colour and texture, and she loves vintage designs in fabric and textile. The flowers, dots and stripes represented in her designs draw from 1950s retro and 1960s colour. Her background in wedding-cake design is reflected in her handknitting and crochet – opulent big roses and pretty, delicate flowers and leaves in yummy coloured yarns that look good enough to eat.
www.laughinghens.com

Amy Twigger Holroyd is the designer of luxury knitwear label Keep & Share, for which she creates unconventional yet wearable pieces, each knitted on a chunky domestic machine in her Herefordshire workshop. Having first studied fashion design, she specialized in knitting, inspired by the potential for seamless three-dimensional shaping and the ability to create fabric and garment in one. Amy was taught to handknit by her grandmother as a child and created many weird and wonderful (usually half-finished) projects. The pattern in this book is her first foray for several years back into the world of handknitting and features a handknit version of her signature joining technique.
www.keepandshare.com

Juju Vail came to the UK in 1990 to study for an MA in Textile Design at St Martins, after studying fashion and knitwear design in Montreal.

Since graduating, she has taught and written books and articles on many creative practices. These include quilting, sewing, beading, knitting, crochet, painting and rug making.

Juju has a whim of iron and chronicles her creative passions on her blog. Her latest book is *Creative Beadwork*.
www.jujulovespolkadots.typepad.com

Donna Wilson graduated from the Royal College of Art, London, in July 2003. During her time there, she produced a range of work that included the 'knitted friendly creatures', the 'doily rug', 'wrapped cacti', the 'caterpillow' and the 'hands on rug'. The tactile quality of her work comes from her childhood in rural Scotland, where she developed a love for the organic form.

Donna's work is playful, tactile and bright, inspired by the everyday oddities and deformities of life. She likes to think of each of her creations as a character in her very own wonderland, where scale and perception are toyed with.
www.donnawilson.com

Acknowledgements

This book would not be possible without the incredible work and involvement of so many people. I wish to express my thanks to all the talented designers who have contributed their creativity and sensibility to this project. The fact that you took time out of your already very hectic lives has truly touched me. From your yarns to your patterns, you are all shaping the world of knitting in a tremendous way.

A big thank you to my editor, Zia Mattocks, who, with her cool head, calmed me down in some of my more panicky moments and kept things ticking over. Thanks also to Barbara Zuñiga, a great book designer with a brilliant eye, who I had the great fortune to have contribute to this project. Thanks to Vanessa Davies, whose beautiful photography has brought the patterns to life. And to Pauline Hornsby, our brilliant pattern checker and technical editor. And of course, Jacqui Small, who thought of the book in the first place – thank you for approaching Loop and believing in the book and making it happen.

Thanks to Blue Sky Alpacas, Designer Yarns, ggh, Rowan, Jade Sapphire, Habu Textiles and Be Sweet for their generosity and support (and for making such great yarns for knitters). Special thanks to Gina Wilde at Alchemy Yarns for making the time to dye her gorgeous yarns in the colours we needed.

My heartfelt thanks to the incredible staff at Loop. I have been blessed, right from the beginning, with warm, responsible, helpful women who happen to be great knitters as well. Thank you to Claire Montgomerie and Linda Marveng. Your grace and enthusiasm have made both the shop and this book a joy to do. Thanks also to Natalie Abbott and our talented teachers at Loop, whose patience, together with their passion for knitting, inspires us all: Aneeta Patel, Laura Long, Juju Vail, Julie Arkell, Bee Clinch, Jane Lithgow and Emma Seddon. Thanks to Emerald Mosley, my brilliant website designer. And also, of course, thank you to all Loop's customers – we wouldn't be here without you.

To my dad, Jack Silverberg, and Joy, who like to mooch around the yarn fairs with me and have always been hugely supportive in numerous ways. And my mom, Joan Podel, Loop's biggest fan, whose enthusiasm has never waned.

I couldn't have done any of this book without the huge support behind the scenes from my dear husband, Steven, and our three children, Sonia, Niall and Jonah. Over the course of a year they have been generous beyond belief and endlessly patient with a sometimes distracted partner and mom.

ADDITIONAL CREDITS

Photograph on page 7 copyright © Simon Brown, reproduced by kind permission.
www.simonbrownphotography.com

The publisher and author would also like to thank the following companies for kindly lending props for the photoshoot:

Grainne Morton
Tel: +44 (0)131 443 2755
www.grainnemorton.co.uk
Beautiful jewellery made with charms in silver casing

Seven & Eight Home
www.sevenandeighthome.co.uk

Sukie
Tel: +44 (0)1273 542 600
www.sukie.co.uk
Lovely quirky notebooks and other paper products

Vintage Heaven
Tel: +44 (0)1277 215 968
www.vintageheaven.co.uk

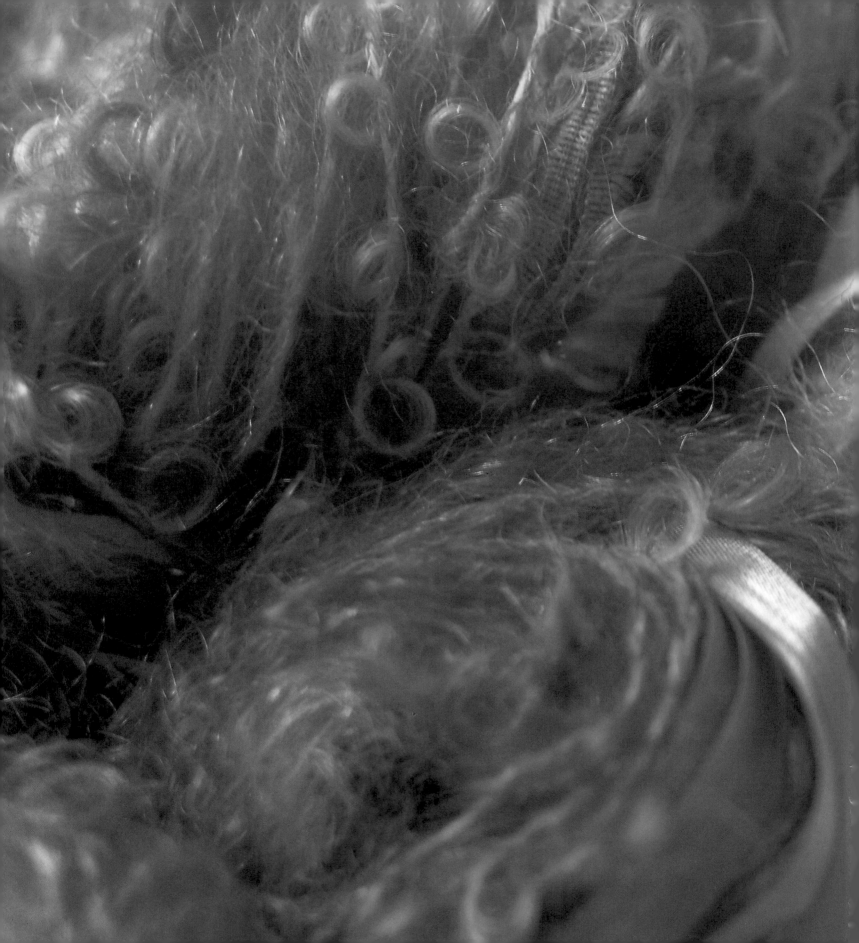